BLIND CHANCE OR INTELLIGENT DESIGN?

Empirical Methodologies and the Bible

———

By Jack Wellman

"There are only two ways that you can live. One is as if nothing is a miracle. The other is as if everything is a miracle.   I believe in the latter"
Albert Einstein

Blind Chance or Intelligent Design? Copyright © 2014 by Jack Wellman All rights reserved. No part of this book may be reproduced or transmitted in any form or by any means without written permission from the author. To contact the author, please email him at: jackwellman@hotmail.com 98 pages ISBN 978-0-557-09307-6
Printed in USA

Table of Contents

Preface: Christian Apologetics: Paul on Mar's Hill   8

Chapter 1 Biblical Manuscripts & the Inerrancy of the Word   15

Chapter 2 Jesus Christ: An Historical Fact   24

Chapter 3 Evidences of the Resurrection   32

Chapter 4 Archeology and the Bible   38

Chapter 5 Jesus' Fulfillment of Biblical Prophecies?   45

Chapter 6 Blind Chance or Intelligent Design?   52

Chapter 7 Probabilities for Life by Spontaneous Generation?   60

Chapter 8 The Moral Argument   68

Chapter 9 The Cambrian Explosion   74

Chapter 10 Missing Links or Fossil Phonies?   79

Chapter 11 Carbon-14 Dating - Accurate or Reliable?   91

Chapter 12 The Universe, Young or Old?   98

INTRODUCTION

This book is a compilation of empirical, scientific, philosophic, archeological, paleontological, historical evidence, intended for home-schooled children, for the graduating high school seniors, for high school students, K-12 students, college students, for the skeptic, the curious and Christians. It is Christian Apologetic's answer to the unproven theory of evolution and scientific hypothesis on the origin of life and the universe. The book examines the hard evidence of what we do have, as opposed to what is assumed. Not only is there missing fossil evidence for mankind, we have no transitional fossils for animals, mammals, insects, other organic life-forms, and plant life. What we do find are plants, already at the flowering stage, appearing suddenly, with no ancestral fossils above or below in the Cambrian period. Just like the majority of life forms as they already appear today. Geologically, they appear suddenly and already fully formed with complete body parts, already complete flora, fauna, appendages, etc. and not in a gradual, progressive, evolutionary pattern.

Apologetics is not an apology for a belief in God, but rather, as the original Greek says, (apologētikos) is suitable for defense. It is the branch of theology that is concerned with defending or proving the truth of Christian doctrines and this means evidence for Creation, for Jesus Christ and His resurrection, and the empirical, quantifiable evidence that the Bible is true, as written. I understand that Apologetics swims upstream in this secular culture: one with the predisposition built on cable TV, movies, the Internet, the History Channel, National

Geographic, PBS, and others that evolution is a given fact. The "facts" manage to do away with the need for a god. The amazing facts about the universe and the scientists who examine them worship the creation and not God. There was a similar culture during Paul's missionary work and in particular the Greeks.

The alleged evidence for evolution will also be examined, even though it is unable to pass the Scientific Method which means it must be observable, repeatable, measurable, and be falsified. Theories have been proven wrong before. The theory of evolution is actually built upon yet more theories; biogenesis and abiogenesis for example. These are further assumptions that are made, hypothesis that support the assumptions and abstract reasoning's which have created a theory for the origin of the universe. In reality humans can only make a subjective "guess" about how life and the universe came into existence; some are now saying it has always existed (Steady State theory) but the beginning is clearly recorded in the Word of God (Gen 1:1-2).

If the universe never had a beginning, then I would ask them one question. Name one thing in the entire universe that will last forever, or one thing that had no beginning. And if all things physical had a beginning, so also must they have an ending. Matter and life are finite. And cause precedes effect.

Anyone who cares to examine the archeological evidence that we presently have, will discover that not even one single set of transition fossils shows up for even one specie evolving into another. And despite the fact that some of the fossils have been exposed as hoaxes, they are still being publicly displayed.

Look at evolution's Tree of Life. Even I can see that a T-rex is not a transitional specie related to the chicken! One fossil or fossilized animal is not a missing link since there remains no chain with which to attach it too. Plant life also reveals no fossilized ancestors, but chiefly an explosion of plant life in the Cambrian strata as archeological evidence reveals. The Cambrian explosion is where most all plant, mammal and animal life appear…suddenly, almost like an explosion with few ancestors below or above. They appear already fully formed, with all appendages, organs body parts and phyla. No one has ever found a set, or even close to a set, of two or even three transitional fossilized remains that shows a progressive evolvement from one life form to the next or even a specie evolving. I believe it is because you will never find what does not exist. I intend to prove this.

For the one who closely examines the scientific evidence, there is a gaping hole or a roaring silence of evidence. Humans have tried for well over one hundred years by experiment to create life. They have never once done it, regardless of the thousands of attempts. The same thing goes for their trying to "boost" evolution along (see the fruit fly experimental failures) by genetic engineering. The managed to have the fruit fly did evolve but to a state that it couldn't fly and thus, reproduce. It ended up having a cumbersome number of wings most tragic, the fruit flies became sterile.

To God, first and foremost, be all the glory, and all the credit. He revealed what I could not see. He closed what I did not need to see. It is a blessing if we can be in God's will. It is an even greater blessing if that is what your passion is. For me, it is to reveal Him as existing but with the realization of doing this in love, gentleness and meekness and not in an argumentative or hotly debated way. I would rather lose a debate and win a soul than win a debate and lose a soul. Jesus told

Peter, and by application, all of us, that the revelation of God and Who Jesus is comes from the Father's prerogative and that the knowledge of God is imparted by God Himself. No one has ever been argued into heaven that I know of. The results of arguing are usually a steadfast defensive entrenchment of the one party and a prideful attitude from knowledge on the Christian's part (I know all too well). It is a lose-lose situation. At the same time, it doesn't hurt to inform people that we have empirical archeological, historical, paleontological, mathematical, philosophical, and scientific evidence to reveal Him as Creator and as the Redeemer but it must be done in a spirit of love, genuineness, and in sincere compassion for the other person, not brow-beating them into a submitting to defeat.

Was Paul the first and greatest Apologist (beside Jesus Christ)? I don't know. His Mar's Hill evangelizing of the Greeks was an inspiration to me. He was willing to risk rejection, the ruining of his reputation, being called a narrow-minded, a despiser of Moses and the Law.

"Then Paul stood in the midst of the Areopagus and said, "Men of Athens, I perceive that in all things you are very religious; for as I was passing through and considering the objects of your worship, I even found an altar with this inscription: TO THE UNKNOWN GOD. Therefore, the One whom you worship without knowing, Him I proclaim to you: God, who made the world and everything in it, since He is Lord of heaven and earth, does not dwell in temples made with hands. Nor is He worshiped with men's hands, as though He needed anything, since He gives to all life, breath, and all things. And He has made from one blood every nation of men to dwell on all the face of the earth, and has determined their pre-appointed times and the boundaries of their dwellings, so that they should seek the Lord, in the hope that they might grope for Him and find Him, though He is not far from each one of us; for in Him we live and move and have our being, as also some of your own poets have said, 'For we are also His offspring.' "Therefore, since we are the offspring of God, we ought not to think that the Divine Nature is like gold or silver or stone, something shaped by art and man's devising. Truly, these times of ignorance God overlooked, but now commands all men everywhere to repent, because He has appointed a day on which He will judge the world in righteousness by the Man whom He has ordained. He has given assurance of this to all by raising Him from the dead." And when they heard of the resurrection of the dead, some mocked, while others said, "We will hear you again on this matter" (Act 17:22-32).

God desires that no one would perish and it occurs to me that evolution does away with the need for a god even though God "Spoke" and things existed. That's what the fossil records show; the (Cambrian) explosion of plant and fossil life that looks to the naked it like it was the creation of all life. It is my desire that you too would share Jesus Christ and Him crucified for others, even by an Apologetic means if necessary, and particularly for the more skeptical like Paul encountered on Mar's Hill and in Romans chapter one and two.

A huge thank you to my mother-in-law, Janet Wilson who took a risk and loaned me money for my first book, printed by a now extinct company that made phone books and also to my loving wife who supported me through the many tedious weeks and months. Most of all to God Who provided the resources and to Him and for His glory this book is dedicated.

Matthew 28:18-20 and in Acts 1:8 contain imperative commands from

Jesus to reach those who don't know Him and make disciples of others and to go into all the world, even if it's too my next door neighbor and by all means possible that at least one might be saved. My hope is that in writing this book, Christians can always be ready to give an appropriate answer for the hope that is in them, or that the non-believer might be persuaded to believe in a creation and thus, believe in the Creator. Hebrews 11:1 says that, "…faith is the substance (or confidence) of things hoped for, the evidence (or proof) of things not seen." Using empirical methodologies in several disciplines, the "substance" and "evidence" to be examined, I hope and I pray, will bring that confidence.

CHAPTER ONE

The Word: Biblical Manuscripts and the Inerrancy of the Word

While I was writing this, I came to a conclusion. It is simply not possible to include all of the evidence that there is about the Bible's veracity. With mountainous piles of manuscripts, different translations, fulfillment of prophecies, historical and archeological finds, and so on, no one book can describe all that there is. Even with the vast amount of empirical evidence of the Bible's unchanging Word, its authenticity, truthfulness, prophetic fulfillments, and that it is the divinely inspired Word of the Living God, there remains room to doubt for some. Even among professing Christians, almost half believe you can't take every word in it seriously or that some things in the Bible didn't really happen. How Christians cannot believe that *all* of the Bible is true is beyond me. The Bible can be examined by empirical methodologies, and it is possible to come to a clear conclusion about it. In latter chapters, historical, archeological, scientific, mathematical, and other methodologies will be used, in an empirical sense; and with tangible, quantifiable results.

When compared to most human historical documents, Biblical manuscripts reign supreme by far. The greatest problem is a good one to have…that there is so much evidence to introduce as exhibit's A through Z in the hundreds…that the case of the Bible being true, would have been solved long before it even started.

New Testament manuscripts have been preserved by the thousands.

No other ancient works or events in human history have what the Bible contains today in documented and recorded histories. There are over 5,700 complete or fragmented Greek manuscripts, 10,000 Latin manuscripts and 9,300 manuscripts in various other ancient languages including Syriac, Slavic, Gothic, Ethiopic, Coptic, and even Armenian.

The dates of these manuscripts range from the 2nd century B. C. up to the invention of the printing press in the 15th century. And every year two or three New Testament manuscripts handwritten in the original Greek format are discovered. The latest large find was in 2008, when 47 new manuscripts were discovered in Albania and at least 17 of them unknown to Western scholars.[1]

Here is a summary of what documents exist today.

Over 24,000 New Testament manuscripts, 5,000 of which date from the first century, which to Historians is a primary source from eye witnesses.

Over 5,600 Dead Sea Scrolls with different authors from the Old Testament, all agreeing textually with each other (about .01% which includes vowel's differentiation, consonant blends, etc. but never affecting the text or the context).

Forty authors in three different languages, covering 1,500 years, with two billion in publication since 1455. The Bible has always been the world's best seller.

Compared to secular human history, we have some seven remaining manuscripts of one of the earliest philosophers, Plato, from around 300 B.C. but the most recent copy of these compositions came 900 years after they were written!

Aristotle has forty nine copies of his writings and the copy that is closest to the time of his living came *900 years* after he had written them.

The foundational evidence for the Bible is based upon 7,000 plus (and growing) manuscripts, many dating from their original writings and many as the originals, like in the New Testament writings. These came from the very same century (prior to AD 100) from which these events took place, not some 900 years after the fact like the false gospels of Judas and Mary were.

There are more than 14,000 manuscripts and fragments of the Old Testament of which are divided into three different kinds:

(1) approximately 10,000 from the Cairo Geniza (storeroom) find of 1897, which date back as far as about A.D. 800.

(2) nearly 190 from the Dead Sea Scrolls finds from 1947 to 1955. The oldest of these dates all the way back to 250 to 200 B.C.

(3) the third type contains, at minimum, 4,314 assorted other copies.

There was a remarkably short interval of time between the last of the Old Testament writings, (400 B.C.) to those of the New Testament (A.D. 70 - 95). Interestingly, the New Testament books validate the Old Testament's existence by the frequent reference to them. It stands to reason that Jesus Himself quoted it since He actually *is* the Word of God (John 1:1-3).

By Jesus and the Apostles quoting the Old Testament, it proves that:

(1) the Old Testament did exist, and

(2) that the Old Testament is an accurate, historical record of the events of past human activities, including ancient Israel (which is also supported by modern archeological digs) and their encounters with God and based upon the common theme of God's Law in having two witnesses to confirm a thing, as to establish it as fact, the two Testaments confirm one another as being true. They are more than compatible, they are mutually inclusive. The short time period between the original Old Testament manuscripts ensures the trustworthiness of the New Testament manuscripts. Historically, the oldest manuscript ever found quoted verses in Numbers: 6:24-26. They date from 800-700 B.C.

The Old and New Testament authors were eyewitnesses of these events. When ancient Historians interviewed eyewitnesses to these events, the overwhelming majority described the events exactly as it was recorded in the Bible. Many of the events, people, places, and customs in the New Testament have already been confirmed by secular historians who were almost contemporaries with New Testament writers. Secular historians like the Jewish Historian Josephus (before A.D. 100), the Roman Tacitus (around A.D. 120), the Roman Suetonius (A.D. 110), and the Roman governor Pliny Secundus (A.D. 100-110) make direct reference to Jesus or affirm one or more historical New Testament references.

The early church leaders also recorded events in the church's history, which included Irenaeus, Tertullian, Julius Africanus, and Clement of Rome, all of which wrote before A.D. 250. Again, they parallel what is in the New Testament with astounding historical accuracy. Even the more cynical of Historians agree that the New Testament is a remarkable historical document. The conclusion is that there is clearly, strong external evidence to support the Bible's manuscript reliability and not only with Historians, but with archeologists, anthropologists, and paleontologists.

For years critics had dismissed the Book of Daniel, partly because there was no evidence that a king named Belshazzar ruled in Babylon during that time period or that a great city like Babylonia existed. However, later archaeological research confirmed that the reigning monarch, Nabonidus, appointed Belshazzar as his co-regent while he was away from Babylon. Forty-five thousand digs at over twenty-five thousand different locations later we find that each dig has supported evidence of the Bible's historical record: Belshazzar is mentioned by name, King's Darius and Cyrus reigned, and the discovering of remains of the Hittite's and Babylonian's civilizations. The archeological evidence, as overwhelming as it is, will have to wait until chapter two.

For the Old Testament, any translation or copying differences were inconsequential. Of the thousands of manuscripts, and pieces of manuscripts, the only discrepancies that existed were vowel related (spelling difference), leaving out one consonant or rearranging certain names or words.[2] One such example had "Jesus Christ" while the other version had it "Christ Jesus." Historically speaking, the number seventy was especially symbolic to the Jew. Moses appointed seventy elders, and there were the seventy scribes whose sole purpose in life was to copy the original manuscript so close as to be identical.

One such practice was that each of these seventy scribes had the other sixty-nine scribes check their writings for error. Each of these seventy scribes reviewed the others writings as well as having the other sixty-nine check their own work. Their methods resulted in such an accurate reproduction of scripture that there was only one error for every fifteen hundred words. This leaves absolutely no room for private interpretation or mistranslation that would affect the context. By modern standards, the accuracy rate is superior to Microsoft's Spelling and Grammar Check (no, it is not perfect since it was of human origin). Under these strict guidelines and conditions, no one can dispute that the translation differences has no effect on the message of the Bible or its general context.

Hard evidence verifies the dating of Matthew's Gospel as far back as A.D. 60. Some of these same scholars argue that Mark wrote the first Gospel, this discovery would push the composition of Mark to within 20 years, at most, of the events his Gospel describes. Taken together, the synoptic Gospels (Matthew, Mark, and Luke) and Luke's second volume, Acts, would give us a record of the events of Jesus' life, death, and resurrection indisputably written within the lifetimes of those who were eyewitnesses. And if it resides in the Bible, then it is a given.

People can be wrong, but how could thousands of people in Jesus' own lifetime all get it wrong and about the exact same thing!? Otherwise, we must conclude that this is the greatest mass-hypnosis of people in history. That thousands all had optical illusions, and all at the same time, is clearly impossible. It's easy to deceive a few people, but to have deceived so many thousands into seeing and hearing exactly the same thing? Thousands have died for belief in Him. We might live for a lie, but how many would die for one and something they know is false?

The Bible's authenticity stands firm, empirically, in archeology, anthropology, and (in the next chapter) historically. Archeology and history has only now confirmed what the pages of the Bible recorded long ago. The Bible we have today was providentially preserved in the past. The rigorous canonization that the church used in protecting and preserving the Bible was the motivation for the written Creed, which is the churches universal Statement of Beliefs. The preservation of the Word (Old Testament and New) serves as sufficient proof for its reliability, it's remaining true to the text and context, and to its truthfulness in what was written.

In the truest sense, the redemptive plan of God's reconciliation of humans to Himself starts in the first chapter of the Gospel of John and not in Genesis. The first chapter of John is actually closer to the beginning of God's plan of salvation since it began before anything was yet created. John wrote in chapter one that the Word existed even before the earth's foundation was laid; in fact before the creation. The "In the beginning" of Genesis one is preceded by John chapter one. Before anything was, the Word was. The agreement of a redemptive plan was decided upon before the creation, with the Word (Jesus) agreeing to become a Man: Fully God and fully Man. How could Jesus have been 100% God and 100% Man at the same time? Well, look at it this way: All Kansans are Americans. But not all Americans are Kansans. But the Kansans are 100% Kansan and are also 100% American. In John One it's says that, "The Word was with God and the Word was God". He became a Man as a means to rescue humans (vv. 1-3) and in order to save humans (John 3:16) He died. Jesus Christ is the literal Word of God: The Logos. The Bible is His Word, and His Word is the Bible. It is an expression of Who He is, How He is, What He is, Why He is and Where He is and When He is (without beginning or end). His certainty is the church's chief cornerstone. I hope that in you knowing that He exists, and in the next chapter, that He is an historical fact, you might understand that He is as sure as tomorrow's sunrise.

1 http://www.christiantoday.com/article/nt.scholar.on.discovery.of.giant.trove.of.bible.manuscripts/18204.htm 2 http://en.wikipedia.org/wiki/Biblical_manuscript

CHAPTER TWO

Jesus Christ: An Historical Fact

Jesus Christ is a fact of history and the Bible is *His*-story but a good many people believe He never even existed, or that He wasn't really resurrected; or that He could not have been born of a virgin; or that the miracles He performed couldn't have really happened however, one thing is certain: Most secular historians admit that Jesus Christ did exist and was an actual figure of history. Regardless of what they believe about Him, most believed that Jesus lived! They cannot explain Him away. There are countless authors and historians, thousands of manuscripts, hundreds of eye witness testimony, all providing a multitude of His experiences on earth.

The great lineage of Jesus Christ is recorded at the beginning of Luke. The names of all these men are historical fact and even the census that Joseph and Mary had to travel to Bethlehem to take was registered in the king's census (Luke 2:1-5). Non Jewish people knew that "He was the very (real) Christ (Messiah)" (John 7:27). Thousands upon thousands of eye witnesses knew Jesus by sight and knew He was the Messiah and was the son of David by lineage (Luke 1:1-18:35-43). Even the Chief Priests, Scribes, Pharisees and Sadducees knew Jesus told the truth and was from God (Luke 20:20-26, 19:28-40, 20:20-26). And in the whole of Judea and Samaria, there were thousands of witnesses (Luke 24:15-24, Act 1:3-4, 2:31-32, 9:3, 17, 1 Cor. 15:4-8, 2 Pet 1:16- 21, John 3:2, 15:27, 1 John 1:1-3, 14) and more than 500 who saw Him after His crucifixion (1Cor. 15:4-8, 9:1).

The Old Testament predicted Christ's coming thousands of years before He actually did (Gen. 18:18, 28:14, Duet 18:15-19, Psalm 122:18, 132:11, 11:1-7, 2:7, Is 53:7-8, 49:6-9, 7:14, Acts 3:22-25, 7:32, Heb 5:5-6) and in fact it describes a crucifixion long before it was even know about (Psalm 22, Is 53, 50:6, 25-29, 49, 52:13-15, 62).

Why would nearly 100 ancient Historians include Christ in their writings if they knew he didn't exist? Josephus, Tacitus, Gibbons, and others (all of which are highly respected) would not have written about someone that they believed was a myth. They wrote with certainty when speaking of Jesus. Even skeptical historians agree that the New Testament is a remarkable historical document and so we can say with authority that the Bible has stronger manuscript support than any other work of classical literature, including Homer, Plato, Aristotle, Caesar, and Tacitus, who all pale in evidential comparison.

It is no accident that Jesus is the most widely recognized, well known and written about Person that has ever existed. You cannot ignore the enormous number of original documents that make up the Canonized books of the Bible. These are the most valued of all sources to Historians (a primary source) in validating past events. The Word of God (the Bible) was inspired by the Spirit of God (2 Tim 3:16-17) therefore His testimony is true. That testimony is that Jesus lived, was buried and then resurrected. He lives today and has lived for eternity. There is an absolute avalanche of evidence for His resurrection, including 500 who were eye-witnesses of seeing Him after His death and burial (1 Cor 15:6). This is not a blind faith but a proven fact.

The Bible is the greatest primary source about Jesus that there is. They are His words and His words are the highest reliability there is and He cannot lie. He has sworn by His Own Name, for there is none higher than the name of Jesus. Evidence continues to build with recent discoveries (2006) like the bones and remains of Caiaphas the high priest, a written reference of King David, and a stone tablet bearing Pontius Pilate's name, Egyptian references of Joseph, and dozens more. The list is still growing. The Bible is the most comprehensively documented (manuscripts), supported (archeologically), preserved (nearly 30,000 manuscripts) compilation of historical records and events ever assembled in all of human history.

Perhaps most people don't believe in Jesus Christ because they think that the only written record of His life is restricted to the Bible and many people see scriptures as less than 100% convincing. In fact, some go so far as to say that He never even existed or He was just a good teacher. This is hard to believe, since even the non-religious or other world religions have heard of Him. And there are enormous amounts of secular history from secular historians who were contemporaries of Jesus and they go into such great detail in writing about Him that they are most convincing. These historians included almost every culture in the world at that time. Here is what they wrote:

Thallus is perhaps the earliest secular writer to mention Jesus in his writings….even though his writings are so ancient, that no copies exist but those of Julius Africanus, who writes around 221AD quotes Thallus. Thallus and Africanus both mention a strange darkness that occurred at the same time of Jesus' crucifixion and these stories of a "strange darkness" were written about far and wide on the earth. They all coincided with around 32-33AD.

Africanus writes that "Thallus in the third book of his histories, explains away this darkness as an eclipse of the sun" although ancient records show that there was no eclipse the year that Jesus dies. This record of Thallus does confirm that Jesus lived, and was crucified and that something highly unusual and unexplainable happened on that day. There were many reports of various earthquakes, destruction, and a "strange darkness."

Africanus also mentions a historian named Phlegon who wrote a chronological history around A.D. 140. In this history, Phlegon also mentions the darkness surrounding the crucifixion in an effort to explain it, but even more interestingly, he mentions Jesus' ability to foresee the future in describing the life of our Savior. Josephus (AD 37 – c. 100), born of a priestly and royal ancestry, survived and recorded the destruction of Jerusalem in AD 70.[3] At age 13, this child prodigy was already a consultant for the Jewish rabbis, by 16 he became a Galilean military commander and a Roman Citizen. Being under the rule of Roman Emperor Vespasian, he was allowed to write a first-century history of the Jews. Being a devout Jew and Roman Citizen, Josephus could hardly be described as a hostile witness. He wrote more about Kings than Messiah's, but Josephus makes references to the Sadducees, the names of Jewish High Priests of the time, the Pharisees and the Essenes, the Herodian Temple, Quirinius' census and the Zealots. He also writes of such figures as Pontius Pilate, Herod the Great, Agrippa I and Agrippa II, John the Baptist, James the brother of Jesus, and of course, about Jesus. He even describes the death of John the Baptist and mentions the execution of James, all of which are described in the New Testament.

People, groups, times and events written about are corroborated in the

New Testament by Josephus' history. He describes the death of John the Baptist, and knew that James was the half-brother of "Jesus the Christ." In his final passage he writes that Jesus was a wise man and the Messiah, and there is a retelling the resurrection story, all of which is described almost exactly the way it is in the Bible. Josephus writes in his Antiquities of the Jews (18.63- 64; 3.3):

"Now there was about this time Jesus, a wise man, if it be lawful to call him a man; for he was a doer of wonderful works, a teacher of such men as receive the truth with pleasure. He drew over to him both many of the Jews and many of the Gentiles. He was [the] Christ. And when Pilate, at the suggestion of the principal men amongst us, had condemned him to the cross, those that loved him at the first did not forsake him; for he appeared to them alive again the third day; as the divine prophets had foretold these and ten thousand other wonderful things concerning him. And the tribe of Christians, so named from him, are not extinct at this day."

The interesting thing is that the historian Origen states that Josephus was "not believing in Jesus as the Christ"[1] and that "he did not accept Jesus as Christ"[2] but Josephus' actually declares Jesus to be Christ (in the Testimonium). The manuscript evidence in support of the iron-clad, "pre-accretions" reference to Jesus in Josephus is very strong and accepted by the great majority of professional historians. Between the New Testament and Josephus, there is no serious reason whatsoever to doubt the historical 'existence' of the Jesus of Nazareth behind those references. All the relevant non-Jewish historical sources of the time mention Jesus! It is nearly universal. Not just in the books, but it was common knowledge about Jesus' life and death among the people. This was not done under cover, but out in the open as much as could be possible. The Crucifixion was done on a hill, and always by a main thoroughfare, for all to see, far and wide. The list is enormous: Tacitus (Annals, AD 115- 120), Suetonius (Lives of the Caesars, AD 125), Lucian (mid-2nd century), Galen (AD 150; De pulsuum differentiis 2.4; 3.3) Celsus (True Discourse, AD 170), Mara Bar Serapion (pre AD-200?), Jewish Talmudic References (AD 300).

Jesus historicity and story became known from the Mediterranean to Africa to Asia-Minor, and into most of the known world at the time. One example was around AD 70, when a Syrian philosopher named Mara Bar-Serapion, writing to encourage his son, compares the life and persecution of Jesus with that of other philosophers who were persecuted for their ideas. He used Him as an example of being persecuted for your belief. The fact that Jesus is known to be a real person with this kind of influence is important. It should not surprise us that Mara Bar-Serapion refers to Jesus as the "Wise King" and was held in high esteem by most of the known-world religions, save Judaism.

Additionally, Suetonius, Pliny the Younger, and Eusebius of Caesarea, who was a third century theologian who used the library in Caesarea for much of his research, wrote about Christians. Tertullian wrote about Christian worship and persecution that is consistent with New Testament accounts. Justin Martyr, a Gentile who lived in Palestine who later became a Christian records the many doctrines of the church, like the Sacraments, Salvation, etc. "Resources for Philo of Alexandria" who was a Jewish philosopher and historian that lived in the first century wrote similar accounts that are found in the New Testament writings.

In all of human history's ancient antiquities, writings and records, none approaches the validity or the documentation of the Bible. Neither has any person in human history, dead or alive, ever had more written about Him than Jesus Christ. As we have seen and read, Jesus Christ is historically indisputable; that He lived, He did many wonders, He died from a crucifixion and for the Redemption of humans (John 3:16). We also know that He did rise again, which makes it possible for us to also be raised some day. These facts are historically incontrovertible.

1 Origen, Against Celsus, i:47

2 Origen, Commentary on Matthew, x:17

3 http://en.wikipedia.org/wiki/Josephus_on_Jesus

CHAPTER THREE

Evidence of the Resurrection

The great lineage of Jesus Christ is recorded at the beginning of Luke. The names of all these men are historical facts; even the census that Joseph and Mary had to travel to Bethlehem to take was registered in the king's census (Luke 2:1-5). Thousands upon thousands of witnesses not only knew Jesus by sight, but they acknowledged that He was the Messiah and related to King David's lineage (Luke 1:1-10, 18:35-43). Even the Chief Priests, Scribes, Pharisees and Sadducees said as much and that Jesus told the truth. Many of these religious rulers knew He was from God but for fear of losing their authority and positions, conspired to kill Him anyway (Luke 20:20-26, 19:28-40, 20:20-26).

In any court of law, witnesses are invaluable. In the whole of Judea and Samaria, as the Bible says, there were several hundreds of witnesses who saw Jesus before and after His crucifixion (Luke 24:15- 24, Act 1:3-4, 2:31-32, 9:3, 17, 1 Cor 15:4-8, 9:1, 2 Pet 1:16-21, John 3:2, 15:27, 1 John 1:1-3, 14). There were also multiple eye witnesses, including a Roman Guard that saw the empty tomb of Joseph of Arimathea, which Joseph had given for Jesus' burial site.

The knowledge of Jesus' crucifixion, burial and resurrection was so important to the early church within three to eight years after His death, a Creed was created. The Creed's purpose was intended to protect these eye witness's accounts and codify their testimonies accurately, both for present and future generations. Within a few years, some churches had already been infiltrated with other doctrines like

Gnosticism. The Gnostics felt it was through knowledge that salvation came and was only for a special few. The Creed announces to everyone publicly that the only way to salvation is through Jesus Christ alone. The Creed has grown in two thousand years, yet its basic tenets have not. It has grown only to resist un-sound doctrines and so has acted as a hedge against heresy and other (false) gospels. The Creed was not written from a blind-faith perspective or suppositions, but from church leaders and witnesses who had seen these things with their very own eyes. Now, most people would live for a lie, but few I believe would die for one.

One of the world's foremost experts in lines of evidence was Dr. Simon Greenleaf, an American attorney and jurist (1783-1853). Greenleaf views the multiple eye-witness accounts of Jesus and His death and resurrection as admissible evidence fit for a court of law.[1] These testimonies in the New Testament are as valid today as they were then; as acceptable as admissible evidence even for a court of law. Not "third party" or as "hear say", but real people who were there.

Hundreds of eye witnesses provide such a strong, supportive written testimony that they would be admissible in a court of law. In fact, they meet or exceed evidential requirements, so much so that Simon Greenleaf saw the martyrdoms, exponential church growth, and the persistent-through-persecution faith of the believers (often, even up to death) as concrete evidence. Simon wrote that it "...as impossible that the apostles could have persisted in affirming the truths they had narrated, had not Jesus Christ actually risen from the dead.[1] It's important to note that eye witnesses can still convene a jury for something that happened decades ago. There is no statute of limitations for murder.

The world's most famous ex-atheist, Anthony Flew, looked at all the other claimed miracles of all other religions in the world, and stated that the difference is that, "Their leaders are buried and still in their graves. Jesus tomb was found empty!"[2] Dr. Thomas Arnold, 19th-century history professor at Oxford, said, "I know of no one fact in the history of mankind which is proved by better and fuller evidence of every sort, to the understanding of a fair inquiret."[3] There are five historical facts about Christ agreed to by nearly all ancient historians: That He lived, died, was crucified, was buried and was seen again, alive, after the resurrection. Even Jewish authorities acknowledge the empty tomb in their histories in school.

Discovery Channel's 2007 special "The Lost Tomb of Jesus" by director James Cameron and presented by Simcha Jacobovici, a Jewish investigative journalist, drags up very old news in declaring this "find." The Princeton Theological Seminary's Bible scholars flatly rejected the claims that an ossuary found in Jerusalem in 1980 is that of Jesus and His family. Those scholars, archaeologists, and epigraphers who presented papers on the Talpoit Tomb all declare that this is not Jesus tomb. Both conservative and liberal theologians and scholars agree that His tomb was commonly known to have been Joseph of Arimathea's. All of the symposium's participants, including its organizer, signed this statement to show their full rejection of the Talpoit Tomb as Jesus' tomb which the Discovery Channel "conveniently" left out of their program, alone with other important facts.

Faith rests on a rock-solid foundation; it is not a blind faith, but one that is grounded in evidence. The old designer of the Golden Gate Bridge is long since dead, but even though he is no longer around, the bridge provided ample evidence that he did exist. We can have faith in that.

These same principles are what the vast majority of theologians, scholars, historians and archaeologists, both liberal and conservative, use in considering the resurrection. Nearly all believe that the resurrection did occur and that Jesus was raised from the dead. They realize that the testimonies of several hundred eye witnesses of these events cannot be treated as inadmissible evidence. That many witnesses simply can't get it all wrong, nor would they be willing to suffer persecution, ex-communication from family and friends, even death, for something that never happened.

God-defined faith is in Hebrews (11:1) as being the "substance (literally "grounded confidence") of things hoped for, the evidence (proof) of things not seen" (Jesus' and the Passion). Webster's dictionary definition of human faith seems perfectly fitting: "allegiance to duty or a person, a strong loyalty," "belief and trust in God," and "confidence in something/someone." Faith involves an act of the will. Faith is a verb (action) not a noun. The tight-rope walker acts on his own belief that he can make it across the tight rope. This faith is so simple a child can follow it. It is not blind faith, but faith that has proof, evidence, substance, certainty, and confidence.

To know how certain and secure one can be in relationship to Him, simply read John 10:28-29. It is a faith that is so priceless and so valuable that no money could buy it, yet incredibly it is absolutely free for the taking and it is for anyone, anywhere, and at any time. He will turn no one away (John 6:37). If you trust in Jesus, someday your resurrection will be a fact too. That is abundantly evident.

Ravi Zacharias [rzim.org] once said that "the fact is the resurrection from the dead was the ultimate proof that in history, and in empirical, verifiable means, that the Word of God was made certain. Otherwise, the experience on the Mount of Transfiguration would have been good enough." The apostle Peter says in 2 Peter 1:19: "We have the Word of the prophets made more certain...as to a light shining in a dark place." He testified to the authority and person of Christ, and the resurrected person of Christ and Christ told Peter and all who would believe, that they too will be resurrected, for God said it, and we can believe it (1 Cor. 6:14).

1 Greenleaf, Simon. An Examination of the Testimony of the Four Evangelists by the Rules of Evidence Administered in the Courts of Justice. In which he emphatically stated: "it was IMPOSSIBLE that the apostles could have persisted in affirming the truths they had narrated, had not Jesus Christ actually risen from the dead." (Simon Greenleaf, An Examination of the Testimony of the Four Evangelists by the Rules of Evidence Administered in the Courts of Justice, p.29).

2 Gary Habermas and Antony Flew. Did Jesus Rise From the Dead? Harper and Row, 1987. (p. XIIIf, 142).

3 Arnold, Thomas. God and the Bible, 1875, as quoted in Arnold and God. Berkley: University of California Press, 1983. Super, (CPW, VII, pg. 384).

CHAPTER FOUR

Archeology and the Bible

Archeology is like looking at a history book underground. You start with the most recent "chapters" then dig yourself deeper. The further you go down in the earth, the earlier the history so that the deeper you go, the further back in history you go. What archeologists, anthropologists, paleontologists, and historians continue to uncover in Asia, the Middle East, Africa and in Europe, are artifacts that are specifically mentioned in the Old Testament and the New Testament.

About every two years, we find another significant find. Besides the discovery of the Dead Sea Scrolls (1947), the famous Moabite Stone (1868), and the Black Obelisk (1845), there are actually hundreds of artifacts that match precisely what is in the Bible. If you include all of the archeological finds that we have collectively, I could not possibly fit these into one book. It is more than fair to say that this is a treasure trove of archeological finds. Dr. Zeliko Gregor mentions a Galilean fishing boat and dozens of other artifacts that are associated with Jesus.[1]

The most documented Biblical event, the world-wide, is described in Genesis 7-8. Flood legends exist in nearly every known culture, people-group, and isolated island nation in the world. Ancient civilizations such as China, Babylonia, Wales, Russia, India, South and North America Indians, Hawaii, Scandinavia, Sumatra, Peru, and Polynesia, and others, all have their own versions of a giant flood. More confirmation of a global flood is from the discovery of a number of Babylonian documents. These Sumerian writings seem to describe the same flood that Noah and his family went through. The Sumerian King's List, for example, lists each king who reigned, and for what periods of time they reigned. Then suddenly, there is a cease of kings but only a mention of a great flood that came. It was clear from the Sumerian King's List that the Sumerian kings ruled for much shorter periods of time after the flood. This corroborates what is written in the Bible. The most striking thing that you will find is that most on this list shows that no one is living to be hundreds of years old anymore. Noah lived to be nine hundred fifty years (Gen. 9:29) but after they flood, the Bible records no one with such a long life span again. This pattern of long life before the flood and shorter life spans after the flood, are also part of many worldwide cultures, nations, and people groups that have been handed down by written and oral traditions.

The 11th tablet of the Gilgamesh Epic is a great example. It speaks of an ark, animals taken on an ark, birds sent out during the course of the flood, the ark landing on a mountain, and a sacrifice being offered after the ark landed. The Story of Adapa tells of a test for immortality involving food, similar to the story of Adam and Eve in the Garden of Eden. Bible archaeology actually began with the early cities of Abraham and the Patriarchs. The initial archeology discoveries occurred closest to Abraham's ancestral home of Ur, which at one time was a powerful city-state of southern Mesopotamia. This great city-state is mentioned four times in the Old Testament. It is presently located in modern Iraq. Ur has been excavated on and off since the 1800s and has already revealed a wealth of information about the pagan culture of Abraham's time and exactly as described in the book of Genesis. Turkey also is replete with ancient history and was a perennial world- power, which revealed itself as the expansive capital city of the Hittite Empire. The ancient capital of the Babylonian Empire covers nearly 3,000 square acres about 55 miles south of current-day Baghdad in Iraq. The ruins include the famous ziggurat structures, remains of the Tower of Babel, and the Palace of King Nebuchadnezzar, which was also recorded in the Scriptures.[2]

In the Daily Mail Reporter (29th June, 2009, Associated Newspapers, Ltd., London, p. 1), an article mentions that the Pope has confirmed that the Apostle Paul's remains were discovered by Archeologists "under the Basilica of St. Paul's Outside the Walls in Rome. Paul was said to have lain in this sarcophagus for almost 2,000 years. The Daily Mail Reporter quotes the Pope saying that "scientists had conducted carbon dating tests on bone fragments found inside the sarcophagus and confirmed that they date from the first or second century." Church historians say that Paul was beheaded in Rome and buried under the streets late in the first century. Ironically, Vatican archeologists uncovered the earliest known image of the Apostle Paul on a fresco inside a catacomb beneath Rome.

David's was one of the single most prolific writers of the Old Testament. In 1994, written references to "The House of David" were found in both the Hebrew and Aramaic languages. The Aramaic writings could very well indicate that they might have been used during the time of Christ and during the early period of the church. This is especially true since Aramaic was spoken widely then, even by Jews of that time including in Jerusalem. This is quite reasonable since Aramaic would have been the language they spoke and read at that time. Dr. Avraham Biran's team of archeologists, working in the Upper Galilee region commented that,

"This is the earliest archaeological mention of King David."[3] The inscriptions also mention part of the Royal lineage of Israel (other Jewish Kings mentioned in the Old Testament).

In excavations near Jerusalem, archeologists uncovered what they believe to be a part of a much larger network of quarries used by King Herod. The Associated Press reported in the magazine, *Israel Travel,* on July 7, 2009, that Israeli archaeologists uncovered an ancient quarry where they believe King Herod extracted stones for the construction of the Jewish Temple 2,000 years ago as reported by the Israel Antiquities Authority. The archaeologists believe the 1,000-square-foot quarry was part of a much larger network of quarries used by King Herod in the city of Jerusalem. Herod was the Roman-appointed king of the Holy Land from 37 B.C. to 4 B.C. and was known for his many major building projects, including the rebuilding of the Jewish Temple. This same Herod is mentioned in the Gospel of Matthew.[2]

After leaving the Temple, the disciples said to Jesus (Mark 13:1-2), "Teacher, see what manner of stones and what buildings are here!" What was Jesus' response? Did He compliment the Temple's splendor and construction? No, Jesus was not impressed, saying, "Do you see these great buildings? Not one stone shall be left upon another that shall not be thrown down." He did not reflect on the Temple's impressiveness, only on its size. He stressed the coming tribulation and signs of His coming as of far greater importance. This fact is not lost that Jesus' words came true, saying "Not one stone shall be left upon another that shall not be thrown down" because the Romans destroyed Jerusalem in AD 70.

The oldest known manuscripts to the date of this book being published are from the seventh century B.C. These were found in 1979 while excavating a burial site just southwest of Jerusalem. Archeologists unearthed three pieces of silver which turned out to be miniature scrolls. Even though it took three years to unroll them and read them, they contained Numbers 6:24-26 directly from the Bible.[3] It's by far, the oldest reference to God that has ever been found by any archeological team. This dig was done by a team lead by Dr. Avraham Biran. Dr. Biran is considered Israel's foremost expert archeologist. What they discovered in 1993 was an inscribed stone, which was part of a larger monument.[4]

With over 45,000 digs at 25,000 different locations, each providing supporting evidence of the Bible's historical recorded, and mentioned Belshazzar by name as well as King's Darius and Cyrus, and the discovery of the Hittite's and Babylonian's civilizations, it should be clear that the connection between the Bible and archeology is crystal clear. Archeology supports what the Bible records and more archeological treasures seem to arrive every year now. There is more archeological evidence being held today than any one person could ever contain in one book and if the Exodus of the Israel from Egypt never happened, then why have the Jews annually celebrated three great festivals, in commemoration of their Exodus (Passover, Pentecost, and Tabernacles) for over thirty five hundred years? That in itself is a testimony of ancient Israel's tumultuous beginnings and in clear remembrance in her name, which means, "The Prince that prevails of God" of which the Bible says of Israel, they "will be without end" (Isaiah 9:6-7).

1 Gregor, Zeljko (Ph.D., Andrews University) is a specialist in Biblical Archeology. He recently wrote several articles for Eerdmans   Dictionary of the Bible (1997). His mailing address: 4766-1   Timberland; Berrien Springs, MI 49103. full article at:http://dialogue.adventist.org/articles/09_3_ gregor_e.htm

2 http://www.allaboutarchaeology.org/bible-archaeology.htm

3 http://www.biblicalarcheology.net/index.php?s=gezer

4 Schmitt, David R. Blessed For Life. Fenton, MO . Copyright, 2009. CTA, Inc. 2009. (p. 6). ISBE 978-1-933234-81-6

CHAPTER FIVE

Jesus' Fulfillment of Biblical Prophecies

What Are The Odds of Jesus' Fulfillment of Biblical Prophecies? I cannot even describe the astronomical odds that just one person could fulfill 300 prophecies written about Him and the vast majority of these prophecies were written thousands of years before He even existed as a Man. The prophecies stretched from Genesis throughout the Old Testament, and for those yet future, in the New Testament. If these were the odds in a lottery, you couldn't possibly win. Most scholars acknowledge that there are possibly seven hundred prophecies or more about Jesus Christ in the Bible. For the sake of being able to wrap your mind around the odds, let's just take eight prophecies. The actual mathematical probability that Jesus Christ could have fulfilled even eight prophecies would still be a mind boggling 1/10 to the 157th power. That's a 1 in 100, 000, 000, 000, 000, and 000. This page would fill up with "0000" if I wrote out what the odds would look like (and it be at least one page with nothing but zero's. That is a number that no one can even fathom. Now imagine the likelihood of Jesus Christ fulfilling seven hundred prophecies by chance.

Now, what are the odds that only 48 of the more than 700 (that we know of) prophecies of Jesus were fulfilled? Dr. Peter Stoner [Science Speaks, 1958] estimated the odds against just 48 of the 300 or so Old Testament prophecies about the Messiah being fulfilled in one Person. He calculated the odds at 1 in 10 to the power 157.[1] This illustrates why it is absolutely impossible for anyone to have fulfilled the Messianic prophecies solely by chance. Emile Borel is a leading authority on the probability theory, and he states in his book *Probabilities and Life*, once we go past one chance in 10 to the 50th power, the probabilities are so small it's impossible to think that it will ever occur.[2] Mathematicians generally agree that, statistically, any odds that go beyond 1 in 1050 have a zero probability of ever happening by random chance. This is Borel's law in action which was derived by mathematician Emil Borel.[3] The necessary conclusion then would be that these prophecies were not mere coincidences; not when you consider the chances at the exponential power that they were at. When the Roman soldiers cast lots for Jesus' garment, another prophecy was fulfilled as, "They divide my garments among them and cast lots for my clothing" which was fulfilled in Psalm 22:18. By the way, the dividing of garments between attending Roman soldiers was completely normal at crucifixions, but casting lots was not. This was illegal and for the Roman soldier while on duty, it was punishable by death! John 19:23-24 might explain why this exception was made. This one seamless garment was of much better quality than normal, so instead of tearing it in pieces so that they could share it, they cast lots for it. Now, what are the exact odds against this exception? This seems to have been a rare event since the soldiers had to discuss how to deal with it. Surely it would be conservative to assign a probability of one in twenty-five. This brings the chances down, relatively speaking, to one in 187,500 of being just a random chance happening.[1]

The subject on the odds for Biblical prophecies coming true is equally astounding, if not unfathomable. There are over 100 prophecies alone about Babylon that have all been fulfilled and some yet remaining in Revelation. In the book of Isaiah, he foresaw the fall of Babylon which would not even emerge as the world's most dominant power for another hundred years. (Isa. 21:1-10) and the Succession of world empires were told, in advance, in Daniel 2 and 7. Tyre's fall was also foretold precisely as it happened in Ezekiel 26. It should be noted that these men actually wrote down God's foreknowledge. Whether it was by the Spirit or they were in the Spirit, I do not know but this I know; God's Word is the authority behind these prophecies and not the prophets. The way in which God addresses these prophets is "Thus says the Lord," which occurs over 3,808 times! This infers that these prophecies are the words of God and not the words of men. The fulfillment of these prophecies by Jesus Christ is quantifiable, tangible, and empirical evidence for the veracity of the Bible.

Here's another example. Jesus was known by many as being from Nazareth. Ironically (or not), Nazarenes' providential arrangements required the parents to live in Nazareth, which was the fulfilling of prophecies in which the Messiah is described as a "shoot" or "sprout" of Jesse and by specific application, Jesus fulfilled the perfection of what a Nazarene should be. They were required to be set apart for service to God at an early age or essentially a self-sacrifice of themselves to His service. This meant that they offered their own lives as an offering to God (normally Levites' duties). They were also to be a monitor or witness of the law (Numb 6:2-17, Lev 21:10-12, Ex 29:2). There are far too many of these prophecies to be covered in one book but here are some of those which Jesus fulfilled in two ways. Foretold in the Old Testament, and fulfilled in the New Testament.

Born of a virgin	Isa 7:14, Matt 1:23
Born in Bethlehem	Micah 5:2, Matt 2:1
Lived in Nazareth	*Isa 11:1, Matt 2:21-23

Rejected by his own	Isa 6:10, 53:1-3, John 1:11
Enters Jerusalem triumphantly	Zech 9:9, John 12:12-19
Betrayed by a friend	Zech 11:12-13, Matt 26:14
Died with criminals	Isa. 53:9 Matt 27:38
Buried with the rich	Isa 53:9-12, Matt 27:57-60
Lots cast for his clothes	Psl 22:18, Luke 23:24
Offered vinegar to drink	Ps 69:21, Matt 27:34
Dying words are given	Ps 22:1, 31:5, Mt. 27:46, Luke 23:46
No bone is broken	Ps 34:20, John 19:36
His side to be pierced	Ps 22:16, Zech 12:10, John 19:34

Thousands upon thousands of witnesses knew Jesus by sight and knew He was the Messiah and the son of David, by lineage (Luke 1:1- 18:35-43). Even the Samaritan Women at the well knew that a Messiah was to come. Difficult as it is to believe, this was common knowledge in Jerusalem especially among the Chief Priests, Scribes, Pharisees and Sadducees. Many of them acknowledged Him as a Son of David...some knew Jesus told the truth and was from God (Luke 20:20-26, 19:28-40, 20:20-26). Incidentally, this generation was the only one in which they could actually blaspheme the Holy Spirit, since they knew better. Everyone should have. In fact in the whole of Judea and Samaria, there were thousands of witnesses (Luke 24:15-24, Act 1:3-4, 2:31-32, 9:3, 17, 1 Cor 15:4-8, 2 Pet 1:16-21, John 3:2, 15:27, 1 John 1:1-3, 14) and more than 500 people that saw Him after His crucifixion (1 Cor. 15:4-8, 9:1).These people must have talked incessantly about this for years and generations, which is the reason that there were no legitimate stories about it being a hoax, save the false witnesses given by the Jews.

The Old Testament confirms Christ's coming thousands of years before (Gen. 18:18, 28:14, Duet 18:15-19, Psl 122:18, 132:11, 11:1-7, 2:7, Ish 53:7-8, 49:6-9, 7:14, Acts 3:22-25, 7:32, Heb 5:5-6) and describes a crucifixion long before such an execution even existed (Psl 22, Ish 53, 50:6, 25-29, 49, 52:13-15, 62) so based solely on quantifiable, mathematical principles, the fulfillment of the hundreds of prophecies by Jesus, and other events, were no mere random chance accidents, or blind luck. No. He was always at the right places at the right time as the Scripture said. Of course, no finite human being could ever possibly pull off such a thing as the fulfillments of all of the Bible's prophecies about Jesus! This takes a Someone Who can, not only predict things thousands of years before, but Who Himself can bring it to pass. The necessary conclusion must be that it was intentionally preordained and intentionally fulfilled.

1 Science Speaks, by Peter W. Stoner. Copyright © 1958, 1963, 1968 by the Moody Bible Institute of Chicago. (P. 333).

2 Borel, Emil (1962), Probability and Life, Dover, translated from the original, Les Probabilite et la Vie, 1943, Presses Universitaire de France.

3 http://www.talkorigins.org/faqs/abioprob/borelfaq.html

* For Nazarenes', providential arrangements required parents to live in Nazareth, which was the fulfilling of prophecies in which the Messiah is described as a "shoot" or "sprout" of Jesse. By application, Jesus fulfilled the perfection of what a Nazarene should be. They were required to be set apart for service to God or essentially a self-sacrifice of them self to His service, they themselves brought the offerings to God (normally Levites' duties) and a monitor or witness of the law (Numb 6:2-17, Lev 21:10-12, Ex 29:2).

CHAPTER SIX

The Universe: Blind Chance or Intelligent Design?

How did everything, including life, come into existence? Was there a Creator or was it merely by chance that everything in the universe, including all life forms, came into existence? The only other option is that everything that exists materialized out of nothing. *Immanuel Kant versus the Princes of Serendip: Does Science Evolve through Blind Chance or by Intelligent Design*? attempts to answer this question. Kant's response is: "Accidental observations, made in obedience to no previously thought-out plan, can never be made to yield a necessary law, which reason alone is concerned to discover. Reason must not approach nature in the character of a pupil who listens to everything the teacher has to say, but as an appointed judge who compels the witness to answer questions that he himself has formulated."[1]

An accidental world, with chance as a mechanism for life forms swims upstream against science's axiom that out of nothing comes nothing. Cause and effect demands some Causer prior to nothingness. Chance, to Kant, was just an excuse for ignorance. Chance is not even a noun, it can do nothing of itself, it has no power to effect, and it's not an x-factor, as many are convinced. Chance is not composed of physical matter. Regardless of those facts, to those who believe in evolution or carry a disbelief of Creationism or Intelligent Design, chance was the x-factor in everything coming into existence, otherwise they must admit that they just don't know how matter, and thus life, came into existence. They simply don't know and can only placate theories (subjective). We should expect science to deal only with facts (objective), approaching things rationally and logically. The Logical Argument was proposed by Jonathan Sarfati, B.Sc. (Hons.) in Chemistry (with condensed matter and nuclear physics papers substituted) and Ph.D. in Spectroscopy (Physical Chemistry). He put forward the Logical Argument for the universe's existence in April 1998 as: Everything which has a beginning has a cause.

The universe has a beginning.

Therefore the universe has a cause.

There is logical evidence that the universe had a beginning. This can be shown from the Laws of Thermodynamics, the most fundamental laws of the physical sciences and the supposed echo left over from the Big Bang (Creation?). Sarfati's proposal uses established scientific knowledge to validate his argument like in the Laws of Thermodynamics.

1st Law: The total amount of mass-energy in the universe is constant

2nd Law: The amount of energy available for work is running out, or entropy is increasing exponentially. Since the total amount of mass-energy is limited, and the amount of usable energy is decreasing (running out), then the universe cannot have existed forever, otherwise it would already have exhausted all usable energy by now. When all usable energy is used, then what is called the 'heat death' of the universe will occur. For example, all radioactive atoms would have decayed, every part of the universe would be the same temperature, and no further work would be possible.

So the obvious corollary is that the universe began a finite time ago with a lot of usable energy and is now running down. Running down implies a beginning. A wood match will quickly burn the sulfur but it will never break down so much as to be recycled into creating sulfur again. This is the same reason that there can be no Steady State theory; one in which the universe has always existed or that it is eternally recycled every trillions years or so. You can recycle aluminum cans but you can never retrieve the original elements, heat, or energy. It's a one way process. I can't retrieve or recycle the light that our lamp has put out last night and put in back into the bulb or the electrical system. The same applies to star light; light that has already pierced deep into the edges (or beyond?) of the universe can never be put back to where it came from or recycled by a collapsing universe. Kinetic energy used is kinetic energy spent…and gone! It is self-evident that things that have a beginning also have an ending. The law of cause and effect provides that the universe could not be self-caused, self-created. Nothing can create itself. Without an outside cause at least equal to or greater than itself nothing can be created. If it created itself it would have had to exist prior to its being created so logically, it would have had to already exist which is nonsensical. To say the universe (and matter) had no cause, caused itself or has always existed, is essentially saying that all matter existed before it came into existence, which is a logical absurdity. If there was nothing and it brought into existence something, then logically there would still be nothing because out of nothing…nothing comes! So there must have been a cause outside of the material universe.

Dr. R.C. Sproul, an extraordinary Theologian and Philosopher (Ligonier Ministries) can put it so much better than I. He was quoted by John

McArthur (gracetoyou.org) as saying that only four options for the origin of the universe are possible.

Option number one, the universe is an illusion, it doesn't exist.

Option number two, it is self-created.

Option number three, it is self-existent and eternal.

Option number four, it was created by someone who is self-existent." [2]

There are no other options. Either it doesn't exist or it created itself, or it always existed, or somebody created it. That's it! Dr. Sproul says that "I have puzzled over this for decades and sought the counsel of philosophers, theologians and scientists. I have been unable to locate any other theoretical options that cannot be subsumed under these four options. That's all you've got."[2]

Then Dr. Sproul says, "Option number one must be eliminated for two reasons." That's the option that says it doesn't exist, it's all an illusion. "First, if it's a false illusion, then it isn't an illusion. If it's a true illusion, then someone or something must be existing to have that illusion. If this is the case then that which is having the illusion must either be self-created, self-existent, or caused by someone ultimately self-existent. So therefore everything is not an illusion."[2] If we assume the illusion is absolute and that nothing does exist, including that which is having the illusion, then there is no question of origins even to answer because literally nothing exists.

The second option is that the universe created itself, which by all logic is formally false. It is both contradictory and logically impossible. Dr. Sproul argues that, "In essence, self-creation requires the existence of something before it exists." What Dr. Sproul is saying is that the universe can't create itself unless it first existed to be able to create itself. In that case you could ask, "What caused the universe to create itself? It would have had to have a greater cause outside of itself, in which case meant it must have had a cause or creator.

Dr. Sproul says a self-created universe is "a logical and rational impossibility," and "for something to create itself it must be before it is. This is impossible...it's impossible for solids, liquids and gases, it's impossible for atoms and subatomic particles, it is impossible for light, it is impossible for heat, it's impossible for God. Nothing anywhere any time can create itself because if it could it would have had to exist before it created itself."[2] Sproul points out that in this scenario, God can be self-existent and not violate logic, but matter can't be self-created. Whether it is the Big Bang theory, scientists are essentially saying that nothing exploded into something, which is a logical impossibility. To retain a theory of self-creation is totally irrational and rejects all logic. Such a theory can be believed but it can't be argued reasonably and can never be established as a fact.

The third option that Dr. Sproul mentions is that the universe has always existed eternally. The Steady State theory states that the universe has always existed and there was not a time when matter did not exist. The major problem with this is that everything we see or know of in the entire universe had a beginning and will have an ending. Planets, plant life, human life, suns...even gigantic galaxies. There is nothing materially eternal in the universe. I once didn't exist, the house I live in....everything there is at one time did not exist, and if it exists now, it will cease to exist in time. There are all kinds of things in this world that once did not exist but do now and things that once did, that no longer exist today. Nothing can be born and have always existed.

The last option is a possibility that is rejected by most scientists even though the other three options mentioned are logically impossible. This last option holds that the universe exists because it was created by Someone who existed before it existed, a pre-existing intelligent power, namely God. Spontaneous generation has been proven impossible over and over. Matter cannot create itself, just like I couldn't have created myself. This only leaves room for an eternal, pre-existing Someone. The purely logical conclusion is that a "First Cause," as Aristotle called it, was this uncaused Causer. A pre-existing, eternal God could account for such a created order. To cling to any theory other than a "First Cause" is to look at the universe's origination as a theoretical equation: Space + Time + Chance = Everything. To the rational eye, this equation looks like; 0 + 0 + 0 = everything! The problem is that space did not cause matter to come into existence, nor did time. Neither can chance influence nor create events. Can being come from non-being or spontaneous generation of matter come from nothing? Can chance actually do anything or cause something to happen? No. Chance is only the likelihood of something occurring. There must be a cause before an effect can occur and a cause logically demands a Causer. This infers a Creator. Like Aristotle's "First Cause." What is puzzling is that random chance is given the status of a cause.

We hear there's a chance for thunderstorms in the forecast, but the forecaster had no power to create the storms. By assigning a decimal to it (i.e., 40%), we assume that the chance will cause the rain. No, it is only the likelihood of it occurring. The storms had a first cause and it was not the forecaster. Chance is powerless. It cannot make something happen or create something from nothing. It is a non-being and besides, it is a noun, not a verb (action). Has anyone ever identified anything in the universe that was uncaused? There is nothing in the universe that we know of that did not have a cause; every physical thing in the universe will have an ending, which infers that it had a beginning.

I met an old intermediate school classmate far from our hometowns in a big city and I thought that's incredible. What are the chances of that? I did not go to this city to meet him nor did chance make this coincidental meeting happen. My old classmate did not come to the same city to meet me. It was by sheer luck or chance that I saw him but chance did not make me go to this city, it did not influence me going there; I did. Besides, my classmate and I had already existed before we had this chance meeting. I was the cause for going to this city just as my friend had planned this trip.

Strictly speaking, chance is only a possibility quotient, a mathematical equation but you have to have numbers to begin with or you can't even write an equation. Since chance is powerless to create or to cause something to happen, we are left with only one possibility; a cause had to have occurred, and this demands the necessity of a Causer. If there was creating is going on, this logically infers intelligence. Looking at matter, from the sub-atomic levels to the far-flung universes, there is reflected in it, organization, not chaos, intelligence, not luck. There is nothing else which can so easily explain the reason for all matter; and all the natural laws of the universe. This also explains the appearance of life, which is covered in the next chapter.

1   http://physics.bu.edu/static/Glashow/barcelona2002.html National Science Foundation.

2   Sproul, Dr. R. C., Defending Your Faith. Excerpts from John   McArthur. Copyright 2009.   http://www.gty.org/Resources/Sermons/90-216

CHAPTER SEVEN

What are the Probabilities for Life?

One question that evolution is outside of its category to answer is: How did life come about? Could there be life elsewhere in the universe? Did life evolve spontaneously? This question has long been pondered in the scientific and philosophical community. Humans have tried for decades to create life in the laboratory, only to have failed miserably. Spontaneous Generation is the theory that holds that life arose by mere chance with the right timing, the right chemicals, proteins and amino acids, and the right environment for such to live.

In 1952 a graduate student in Chicago attempted to emulate prebiotic conditions on a young earth "billions of years ago" but organic life and DNA were never "created."[1] What biochemists cannot do given almost unlimited funding, time, and contact with the brightest and best scientific minds in the world even with a "simmering, primordial stew" is to create life. There have been several other simulation experiments over the years, yet not even one time, has anyone, anywhere, ever been able to make the sugar-like molecules dioxy-ribose and ribose necessary to build DNA and RNA molecules."[1]

Random chemical reactions are not what any biochemist would bet on when making something as detailed as DNA, even in the fullness of this time of incredible scientific knowledge. Even so, they have tried countless times to produce life and found it impossible to do so. Some of the most recent discoveries have added even more difficulties to the "primordial stew hypothesis." Thus, the origin of DNA/RNA continues to remain one of the greatest and potentially unsolvable scientific mysteries and science has never proven nor do they hold a formula for the purely, random chemical explanation that attempts to answer the origin of the complex DNA molecules necessary for life. By the mid-19th century, so much evidential support had been accumulated, primarily due to the work of Louis Pasteur and others, that the theory of spontaneous generation had been effectively disproved. Pasteur himself remarked, after a definitive finding in 1864, "Never will the doctrine of spontaneous generation recover from the mortal blow struck by this simple experiment."[2] The collapse of spontaneous generation, however, left a vacuum of scientific thought on the question of how life had first arisen. So this community turned to Biogenesis.

Biogenesis, which Pasteur believed was true, is the process of life forms producing other life forms, like a spider lays eggs, which develop into spiders.[3,4] The term is also used for the assertion that living matter can only be generated by other living matter, in contrast to the hypotheses of abiogenesis which hold that life can arise from inorganic (non-living) matter under suitable circumstances, although these circumstances still remain unknown.

Abiogenesis, on the other hand, deals with the origin of life; it's the study of how life on Earth emerged from inanimate organic and inorganic molecules. Scientific research theorizes that abiogenesis occurred sometime between 4.4 and 3.5 billion years ago. By 2.4 billion years ago the ratio of stable isotopes of carbon ($12C$ and $13C$), iron ($56Fe$, $57Fe$, and $58Fe$) and sulfur ($32S$, $33S$, $34S$, and $36S$) pointed to a biogenic origin of minerals and sediments and molecular biomarkers that indicated photosynthesis.[4] This sounds a little like Goldilocks having to have everything "just right" before it would ever happen. Never mind that scientists have tried countless times in vain to replicate these conditions. Abiogenesis is a limited field of research despite its profound impact on biology and human understanding of the natural world. Progress in this field is generally slow and sporadic, reasons being that it depends upon a disproved theory (spontaneous generation) to be true.

Until the 19th century, it was commonly believed that life frequently arose from non-life under certain circumstances, a process known as spontaneous generation. This belief was due to the common observation that maggots or mold appeared to arise spontaneously when organic matter was left exposed. It was later discovered that under all these circumstances, commonly observed life only arises from the replication of other living organisms. Any example can be found in any bachelor's refrigerator; usually a science experiment to itself.

Louis Pasteur thought that bacteria could not develop this way (by spontaneous generation), like in sealed containers, because the life force could not get in. When the theory of spontaneous generation was finally laid to rest in 1859 by the young French chemist, the French Academy of Sciences sponsored a contest for the best experiment either proving or disproving spontaneous generation. Pasteur's winning experiment was a variation of the methods of Needham and Spallanzani. Pasteur had both refuted the theory of spontaneous generation and convincingly demonstrated that microorganisms are everywhere, including in the air we breathe.[5]

Since scientific experiments have failed so miserably in reproducing spontaneous life, the possibility was assessed mathematically impossible. Few are as expert in this field as Dr. Harold Morowitz from Yale University, who is a theoretics expert. Dr. Morowitz deals with the laws of large numbers and probabilities. Here is how the probabilities theory works. You take a set of circumstances, and you scientifically determine the odds of a certain outcome. For instance, if you flip a coin, you have even odds of heads or tails. The more you flip it, the greater the odds are against it coming up heads every time. Once you get to 1/1015, the probability of an event ever happening is negligible. This is what Dr. Morowitz is saying. If you get to 1/1050, the event could not have happened even once in 15 billion-years.[6]

After studying the complexity of a protein molecule, Dr. Morowitz made the conclusion that the probability of life occurring by chance is 1/10236.[6] The odds are so hard to get your mind around that 1/10236 takes into account all the atoms in the universe, and the chance that every one of these, just the right time and just the right ones came together, they just *might* form one single protein molecule. And one protein molecule of itself is dead unless another is formed quickly and we have already seen those odds (1/10236). Dr. Morowitz says that the universe would have to be trillions of years older, and trillions of times larger, for a protein molecule to have occurred merely by random chance. The odds Dr. Morowitz is talking about is like throwing 4 billion pennies into the air and having every last one end up heads. Scientists and even some evolutionists tell us that given enough time, this could happen but as we just learned, there hasn't been enough time and there aren't enough pennies. The odds are so overwhelming as to be impossible however, by this same infinite stretch of logic, many of those same scientists say that a DNA molecule containing four billion bytes of perfectly arranged information did not come from a source of intelligence. It just "happened!" Ruhla's "Physics of Chance" deals with how to derive the predictions of quantum theory. The quantum theory also deals with probabilities.[7]

The biological aspect of life originating on its own also seems just as impossible as the appearance of male and female. Dr. Larry Anderson, a Wellington, Kansas physician, told me that he "cannot see how the male and female sexes evolved or developed separately without the specie going extinct." How is it possible that the species' male and female sex organs were evolving, separately and at the same time, yet still being dependent upon each other to continue the species and prevent extinction?

Anyone who has ever looked at a high school or college science textbook has noticed that the odds for life arising on its own are never mentioned but to believe, without evidence, that every living thing came into existence by improbable random chance and by its environment, is like believing that a perfect dictionary came out of a gigantic printing press explosion. Anything that humans have ever created is the result of a designed product; one which points to a designer. The design argument is literally as old as the hills, but how can the skeptics conquer the counter-intuitive certainty: that information assumes intelligence and intelligence assumes a mind and a mind infers a personage. If you were to walk around on another planet and see stones in a perfect triangle, you could possibly assume that it all came together over eons of time by chance but if you were to come upon a Wal-Mart shopping bag, you most certainly would not say, "Hey, look what the atmospheric pressure has done here." This is because information assumes intelligence.

It is actually better called the "argument to design," the original information density in the ordered human, plant, and animal kingdom. Evolution simply cannot explain the information order of the human cell. Order has not evolved on its own. There is enough information in a single thread of human DNA to fill 600,000 pages of information. That is specified complexity, not just aesthetics. More genetic information can fit on the head of a pin than all the libraries in the world can contain. Thomas Edison was one of the world's greatest scientists, and he said "We do not know a millionth of one percent about anything." Let me repeat: Let's say that you have an incredible one percent of all the knowledge in the universe. Would it be possible, in the ninety-nine percent of the knowledge that you haven't yet come across, that there might be ample evidence to prove the existence of God? If you are reasonable, you will be forced to admit that it is possible. Somewhere, in the knowledge you haven't yet discovered, there could be enough evidence to prove that God does exist.

One scientist has remarked that the possibility of the human enzyme and our chemical makeup coming together by accident is one in ten to the 40,000th power. Ten to the 40,000th power is more than all the atoms in all of the known galaxies of the universe. Any mathematician understands that when you reach that level of improbability, then it can be reasonably stated that it could never happen by random chance therefore it must have been intentionally designed and if there is design, it stands to reason that there must be a Designer with a purpose. Stephen Hawking, a well-known pro-evolutionist once publicly stated that, if we knew the "why" of life, we would know the mind of God. For those who know it was an Intelligent Designer, the question of the "why" of life, has already been answered (John 3:16).

1 Kerr, R. A. October 6, 2006. Has lazy mixing spoiled the primordial   stew? Science 6, 314:36-37. (p. 36, 37).

2 Oparin, Aleksandr I. (1953). Origin of Life. Dover Publications, New York. pp. p.196. ISBN 0486602133.

3 http://en.wikipedia.org/wiki/Spontaneous_generation]

4 http://en.wikipedia.org/wiki/Biogenesis

5 http://en.wikipedia.org/wiki/Abiogenesis

6 Coppedge, Dr. James F. Quoting Dr. Harold Morowitz, Yale   University, in Molecular Biology and the Laws of Chance, 1993.   Published by Probability Research In Molecular Biology.   Northridge, CA 91321 (p. 77)

7 Ruhla, Dr. Charles 1992 [1989]. The Physics of Chance e. G. Barton, translator. Oxford: University Press. (P. 152–203).

CHAPTER EIGHT

The Moral Argument

C.S. Lewis, a former atheist, plainly says, 'If the solar system was brought about by an accidental collision, then the appearance of organic life on this planet was also an accident, and the whole evolution of Man was an accident too. If so, then all our present thoughts are mere accidents—the accidental by-product of the movement of atoms. And this holds for the thoughts of the materialists and astronomers as well as for anyone else's. But if their thoughts—i.e. of materialism and astronomy—are merely accidental by-products, why should we believe them to be true? I see no reason for believing that one accident should be able to give me a correct account of all the other accidents. It's like expecting that the accidental shape taken by the splash when you upset a milk jug should give you a correct account of how the jug was made and why it was upset.'[1]

The "Moral Argument" for C. S. Lewis is as follows:

1.) If God does not exist, objective moral values and duties do not exist.

2.) Objective moral values and duties do exist.

3.) Therefore, God exists.

Now this is a logical reason, since 3 follows necessarily if premise 2 is true. Premise 2 seems intuitively obvious to most people. Mass murdering is unequivocally, objectively wrong. Killing innocent children, torturing animals are all objectively wrong to most people. This is a universal moral. These morals exist universally, worldwide. So if anyone denies premise 2, they don't need an argument, they need help.

The evolutionary explanation strips morality from humans and reduces it to mere descriptions of animal behavior or conduct, a simple physiochemical reaction of the brain's cognitive functions. Darwinists can only explain past conduct and past behavior. It cannot inform or predict a human's future behavior. It only serves to reduce morality to mere descriptions of behavior, which involve both motive and intent. Both of these behaviors are nonphysical elements that cannot, even in principle, evolve in a Darwinian sense. So where do morals come from? Why do they seem to apply only to human beings? Are they the product of chance? What world view makes sense out of morality? Why are babies born with what developmental psychologists call an intrinsic compassion (one baby cry's in the nursery and the others join in). Moral laws suggest a moral Lawgiver; one who communicates through higher, moral principles and laws. For example, most people would not murder someone. They deem this to be morally wrong. Most people expect imperatives to be obeyed or certain consequences occur. Danish philosopher Soren Kierkegaard pointed out that a person could not have anything on his conscience if God did not exist. Kierkegaard cites Genesis, where Abraham is commanded by God to kill his son Isaac. Although God must be obeyed, murder is immoral (it is not technically against the Mosaic Law since it had not yet been delivered—but no matter, it is against our conscience). The ethical is thus suspended for a higher goal (telos).[2]

Morality is grounded in our hunger for justice. We desire for a day when all wrongs are made right, when innocent suffering is finally redeemed, and when those who miscarriage justice, are found guilty and are finally punished. Young children best exhibit this when they say, "That's not fair!" or "I'm telling!" This tendency is from an internal locus of control that already knows right from wrong. This also explains our own personal sense of dread when we feel guilty over something that we now regret, as most people do. The person may feel the need to take the initiative and go make it right by apologizing.

Robert Wright offers no empirical evidence whatsoever for his thesis. He seems to assume, as do most evolutionists, that moral qualities are in the genes; otherwise this paradigm will not work but these are the same evolutionists that are telling us that there isn't any "intelligence" in the DNA information. So now we are to believe that random physiochemical processes now include a conscience of morality? As written earlier, information assumes intelligence.

Take Mr. Wright's comment as an example: "Human beings are a species splendid in their array of moral equipment, tragic in their propensity to misuse it, and pathetic in their constitutional ignorance of the misuse."[3] Mr. Wright reflects on the moral equipment randomly given to us by nature, and then bemoans our immoral use of it with words like "tragic," "pathetic," and "misuse."

If you ask evolutionists about the origins of life, they simply don't know what to say except that maybe life emerged on planet earth as a result of extraterrestrials, or life-ingredients came to earth from space but this just pushes the question back to, "Then where did that life come from?" You have to keep going back to the origin of life, sometime.

One notable challenge to the transcendent nature of morality for biological evolutionists is what is called the new science of evolutionary psychology. Its adherents advance a simple premise: The mind, just like every part of the physical body is a product of evolution. Everything about human personality, marital relationships, parental love, friendships, dynamics among siblings, social climbing, even office politics, can all be explained by the forces of neo- Darwinian evolution. But then how is anyone responsible for anything?

Even the moral threads that make up the fabric of society are said to be the product of natural selection. Evolutionists would have us believe that morality can be reduced to chemical relationships in the genes chosen by different evolutionary needs in the physical environment. Love and hate; feelings of guilt and remorse; gratitude and envy; even the virtues of kindness, faithfulness, and self-control can all be explained mechanistically through the cause and effect of chance genetic mutations and natural selection. They have reached so broad of a conclusion now that they (almost arrogantly) say that all of the moral universals held in the world (including a conscience, morals, etc.) are the result of simple, physiochemical reactions but if these are simply chemical reactions, then taking a human life is just part of the natural, evolutionary order of things isn't it!? It's not the brain's fault. It's a chemical-thing. One wonder's if a high school students chemistry lab results are conscience about anything that the students are doing to them; particularly since chemical mixtures might be able to produce certain "universals." With more humans now dying from abortion than in all of the world's wars this must be okay: Its only "chemistry." To compare life's infinite value to just a simple mixture of chemical compounds, and being at the right place and at the right time, it would be harder to hold a serial killer responsible wouldn't it? Society already defines, legally, when something is called "life" and when it is expedient to dispense with. It is through no fault of his or hers. They are a victim of their brain chemistry or a bad childhood with their parent's bad chemistry.

Evolutional theory states that it's all about survival of the fittest, making decisions based solely on self, and the human species benefiting from any given situation, even at the expense of other "carbon units" however, moral universals point to a Creator; to a Moral Lawgiver. You do not have these unless you receive them and universal morals require an original impartation. Humans are born with universal morals and values that are intrinsic at birth. Moral, values, and character seem more than just a random chemical reaction in the brain; they seem to suggest a Great Moral Lawgiver.

1 C.S. Lewis (1898–1963), The Business of Heaven, Fount   Paperbacks, United Kingdom. 1984. (p. 97).

2 D. Anthony Storm's Commentary on Kierkegaard Second Period: Indirect Communication (1843-46) Fear and Trembling. ©Copyright 1996-2009, D. Anthony Storm   Supplemental source: http://www.sorenkierkegaard.org/kw6a.htm

3 Robert Wright, The Moral Animal Why We Are the Way We Are: The   New Science of Evolutionary Psychology. 1994. New York: Pantheon Books. (p. 23).

CHAPTER NINE

The Cambrian Explosion: Archeological Evidence Against Evolution

What does the actual archeological evidence show that would support, in any way, the theory of evolution when so-called scientific belief has remained a theory for well over one hundred years? It is obvious that it lacks conclusive evidence. If science cannot provide supportive evidence for evolution, perhaps the earth's archeological record of fossils could.

One of the first things unearthed is the division between 'Cambrian' rocks and other catastrophically deposited fossil-bearing rocks. For example the kinds of creatures found fossilized in 'Cambrian' rocks once inhabited the same earth at the same time as those kinds found fossilized higher up the 'geological column.'

Archeologists, paleontologists, evolutionists, and curators of the world's greatest Natural Museums of History have long pointed out the problem for the theory of evolution, namely that all the major groups (phyla) of life which we know today appear in the Cambrian strata with no evolutionary ancestors. This is why evolutionists refer to it as an "explosion" of evolution. There are no groups which have been identified as ancestral to any of the phyla and geologically these phyla seem to have appeared suddenly and simultaneously. The evolutionary conundrum is this absence of ancestors. Each of the phyla represents a basic blueprint, or unique body plan. Evolution's deepest paradox is that in rock layers above the Cambrian no new or different body plans appear. Why not? Why haven't we seen any new animal body plans continued to crawl out of the evolutionary cauldron during the past hundreds of millions of years? According to evolution theory, enormous and radical evolutionary changes have taken place in this time and evolution has not ceased today so why haven't we seen any new body plans? That is something that evolutionary biologists are still trying to determine, since they cannot explain the absence of new body plans that should have been appearing during the past "half a billion" years?

One example is the starfish which has shown no evolutionary changes. It has hundreds of tiny feet which it uses to move along by pumping water through a system of tubes. This is a method we call hydraulics which humans use in machinery. The starfish, which is found fossilized in the Cambrian rocks, has not changed at all. There is no physical evidence the starfish has evolved at all! When we look at fossils in Cambrian rocks, we find that not only did these animals have no ancestors but all the main kinds of living creatures were already there. There were animals with backbones (fish), as well as those without backbones, like shellfish, crinoids (sea lilies), and starfish. Some of these Cambrian creatures have died out, but many are still alive, and have not changed at all.

So why don't we find fossils of the ancestors of Cambrian animals? Evolutionists often say it is because the creatures they evolved from were too soft to fossilize but this excuse will not do. Jellyfish are some of the softest creatures of all, and yet they have been found fossilized. The most sensible reason why we don't find transitional fossils of the ancestors of the Cambrian creatures is that they never existed!

The entire set of unique body plans ever created is represented in all rocks bearing substantial numbers of animal and plant fossils in the Cambrian period. Many of these are now extinct, and are not considered primitive ancestors to todays, but are complex creatures in their own right. No trace of evolutionary ancestors in the transitory fossil records, including in the Cambrian, have ever been found. There is not one single set of transitional fossils of any kind of species that has ever been found in all of archeological history.

Since 95% of all known fossils are of invertebrates, do these same invertebrates appear gradually? Absolutely not, they appear in the Cambrian and in an already fully mature state. There is actually more evidence against evolution than for it. Take Worm Burrows, which have been found in rocks that dated 1.1 billion-years-old. These complex worms are still around today and they have not changed at all from the Cambrian period. There have been no changes in their DNA, in body parts or in their structure...in 1.1 billion years!

The most abundant life on earth is thought to have originated in the oceans. Going from single-celled organisms, to single-celled colonies to colonial organisms (like sponges), then eventually to some fish-like organism. However, transitional fossil evidence has never been found to support this hypothesis. If fish evolved and gradually grew legs to walk out of the ocean, I think it strange that there is no fossil evidence of this. Then, they were supposed to have developed complex lung structures, but again, there is no archeological record of it. There was supposed to be a leap from Amphibian to Reptiles to Birds yet the fossil records for this theory are absent and nothing in the fossil records has ever been found to support this assumption. The outer membranes were supposed to evolve to reptiles' scales then were to have advanced into bird's feathers, and later into fur and then into hairs but again, there is no fossil evidence for this theory. Faulty assumptions lead to faulty conclusions?

The fossil evidence for plants is just as invisible. There is still not one single set of fossil series that has been discovered that is needed to support the phylogenetic trees that are supposed to explain the origin of plant life. Assumptions must prop it up this theory since the fossil evidence can't support it.

Evolution has never once been observed in a science laboratory or by experimentation so it lacks testability and repeatability to establish it as a scientific fact. It also lacks support in the archeological records. The scientific axiom is that cells reproduce cells but my question is "Who produced the first one!?" Could it produce its own self? In my humble opinion, time spent looking for a "missing link" seems pointless when the Cambrian explosion reveals that the entire chain is missing!

CHAPTER TEN

Missing Links or Fossil Phonies?

Author, writer, and paleontologist Luther Sunderland was struck with the same problem that has haunted the theory of evolution from the very beginning; even back to Charles Darwin's day. The claim that one piece of an enormous jigsaw puzzle represents a 500 piece set which happens not only to be missing, but one is which no other piece has been found. The archeological record shows that there is a complete lack of transitional fossils for at least one single set of species. With an estimated 100 million species on earth and another estimated 300 million fossils in private and public collections, no one has yet found a single set of transitional fossils. This lack of conclusive fossil evidence pertains not only for animals, but mammals, the plethora of organic organisms, and all plant life. If, as evolution claims, that plants evolved too, why do most of the earth's flora and fauna appear instantaneously in the Cambrian explosion: And already found to be fully in their flowering and seed stages and they have not changed at all!

If evolutionists, scientists, archeologists, paleontologists or anthropologists cannot find and fill in the missing gaps in the fossil records, they turn to abstract reasoning. This in turn moves to analytical thinking, then to the hypothetical stage, culminating into a theory. These theories, in general, depend upon other theories to be true. Theories have inherent problems; that of being highly subjective which also means that they are subject to error. Laws on the other hand are objective, like the Three Laws of Thermodynamics. These are grounded in objective, observable, measurable ways. Laws are not dependent upon theories; indeed they can invalidate theories. The chief concern for evolution is that there remains no transitional fossil evidence to support it. There is nothing tangible, only theoretical assumptions. Anyone has yet to find a single set of transitional fossils, or even two or three fossils in transition.

The technology is available today, underground imaging, along with human and natural activities; excavations for construction, mining, flooding washouts and so on. We can now dig deep into the earth than ever before, but it is what we haven't found that is the conundrum for evolution, not what we have found. It's the same thing that Darwin was deeply trouble with; a lack of any kind of transitional fossil evidence.[1]

In Charles Darwin's day, paleontology was in it's infancy as a scientific discipline but now, after one-hundred-and-fifty years of looking, we still lack what is required for this theory to be true: Sufficient evidence of transitional fossil records. David B. Kitts. PhD (Zoology) is Head Curator of the Department of Geology at the Stoval Museum stated that, "Despite the bright promise that paleontology provides a means of "seeing" evolution, it has presented some nasty difficulties for evolutionists, the most notorious of which is the presence of "gaps" in the fossil record." Dr. Kitts admits that "evolution requires intermediate forms between species and paleontology does not provide them."[2]

When Mr. Sunderland asked to see the transition fossils from the world's greatest natural museums, they became a bit defensive. In fact, they were sometimes belligerent. Mr. Sunderland started his search with interviews with the five most respected museum officials in the world. Each are recognized authorities in their individual fields of study. These included representatives from the American Museum, the Field

Museum of Natural History in Chicago, and the British Museum of Natural History. The fact is that not one of the five officials was able to offer a single example of a transitional series of fossilized organisms that document the transformation of one kind of animal or plant into another.[3] Aren't the greatest of the world's natural fossil museums where you would expect them to be found? With all the placards about evolution and fossilization in the museums, they must have some on display, right? It's natural to assume that any transitional fossils would on public display and at the world's most prestigious museums.

Mr. Sunderland's first stopped at what is called the King of Fossils! The King of Fossils happens to be the British Museum of Natural History. This museum holds the largest collection of fossils in the world. Mr. Sunderland managed to interview the five most respected museum officials, perhaps in the world. The first and foremost is considered to be Colin Patterson, Senior Paleontologist at the British Museum and editor of a prestigious scientific journal. Dr. Patterson is a well-known expert having an intimate knowledge of the fossil record. Even so, he was unable to show even one single example of Macro-Evolutionary transition in the entire museum.

Mr. Patterson wrote a book for the British Museum of Natural History called "Evolution 2." After examining the book, Mr. Sunderland wondered why there was not even a single photograph of a transitional fossil in it. Mr. Patterson flatly said: "I fully agree with your comments on the lack of direct illustration of evolutionary transitions in my book. If I knew of any fossils, I would certainly have included them. You suggest that an artist should be used to visualize such transformations, but where would he get the information from? I could not, honestly, provide it, and if I were to leave it to artistic license, would that not mislead the reader? I wrote the text of my book four years ago. If I were to write it now, I think the book would be rather different. Gradualism is a concept I believe in, not just because of Darwin's authority, but because my understanding of genetics seems to demand it. This is despite the fact that no gradualisms have ever been found in the archeological record.

Stephen Jay Gould (1941-2002) at the American Museum of Natural History, one of the most influential paleontologists and evolutionary biologists of the late 20th and early 21st centuries was, like Mr. Sunderland, deeply troubled with the philosophical problems of identifying ancestral forms in the fossil record. You say that I should at least 'show a photo of the fossil from which each type of organism was derived.' I will lay it on the line - there is not one such fossil for which one could make a watertight argument."[3] N. Heribert Nilsson, a famous botanist, evolutionist, and professor at Lund University in Sweden, continues: "My attempts to demonstrate evolution by an experiment carried on for more than forty years have completely failed. The fossil material is now so complete that it has been possible to construct new classes, and the lack of transitional series cannot be explained as being due to scarcity of material. The deficiencies are real, they will never be filled."[4]

In 2009, a new "missing link" was announced in New York City amid much hoopla. It was dubbed Ida but it has apparently been altered and even partially fabricated. In the first place, this is not a new discovery at all. Ida has actually been in human hands for over twenty-five years. It most certainly comes with great controversy. The Norwegian paleontologist Jørn Hurum of the University of Oslo Natural History

Museum said at the 2009 New York Press conference, that it's not really an anthropoid, but he but still refers to Ida as coming from the period that's called the Old World Monkeys, about the time that it is thought that humans split off from the gorillas and chimpanzees.

Ida has been the most recent claim as the new "missing link," a claim that was hailed as "changing everything." The History Channel produced a show in 2009 that boasted about Ida as "The Link: This Changes Everything," but what has really changed? The trust is that Ida has been tampered with by humans and precious little is said about the fact that this fossil's been around since 1983, so it is certainly no new discovery. The original owner of the fossil, for some reason, cut it in half. The collector eventually sold both parts and on separate plates to different parties but there are more issues about Ida that the History Channel conveniently left out of their program. A part of Ida was restored and another part was "fabricated" so that it would look "more complete."[5] Scientists wanted to know what was used to "fabricate" it and what was used in the process of it being restored? They also want to know what substances have been added to it for displaying purposes.

Robert Bazell, [The Daily Nightly MSNBC.com 5/19/09] Chief Science Correspondent, quoted the renowned paleontologist Tim White [University of California, Berkeley] who said that it will take years to determine if this is the "Mother of all Monkeys."[5] Paleontologists are highly suspicious of this "missing link."[6] The report says that it will take years of scientific examination before any judgment can be made but as far as the scientific report is concerned, no claim is made that it is a missing link or a fossil that is revolutionary in stature nor are there any sensational claims, like at Ida's press conference, that this fossil changes everything or that is the new "missing link."

Jenz L. Franzen, one of the scientists in the study, showed that some of the specimen is real, while substantial parts were faked in order to give an illusion of greater completeness. The report clearly said that "parts of plate B were faked, including notably, the hands and feet (where some proportions of constructions may have been based on reversed photos of A) and so too was the tail vertebral column. Traces on the surrounding polyester resin background suggest that a cast of the tail of another mammal was inserted into plate B. Additional parts such as the vertebrae between sections 1 and 2 as well the nasal part of the skull on plate B were simply fabricated."[6] This fossil has been so tampered with that it cannot be claimed to be a reliable source for evolution because so much of it has been fabricated, much like the theory of evolution has been.

Remember that these kinds of claims have been made many times and been exposed as frauds. Dozens of the so-called "missing links" have turned out to be absolute fakes. One example was discovered in 1922 that changed the nation's public school system forever. A so-called scientist claimed to have found the true "missing link" between men and animals in Nebraska. Dubbed the "Nebraska Man," it was flaunted in text-books and museums of the world as being one million years old. Pictures and models were created, based on the "scientific" studies of experts. Just three years later, in the famous "Monkey Trial" in Dayton, Tennessee in 1925, it was introduced to prove evolution and show that "ignorant Bible-believers" were wrong! Great "scientific experts" were quoted to prove their case and all who were dumb enough to believe that God created man in His image were mocked and ridiculed! This is the same "evidence" that was used in the Scopes Monkey Trial and insisting that evolution is now a fact of science and thus, should be taught in the public schools. Once again, faulty assumptions can lean to faulty conclusions. And this faulty one had enormous implications.

When evidence of the "Nebraska Man" was demanded, the "great scientific experts" reluctantly admitted that their evidence consisted of *one single tooth!* But that's not all! After evolutionists and the mainstream media reporters bullied lowly Bible believers for years with their "scientific proof" the rest of that skeleton was found, and guess what? It was the skeleton of an extinct pig! There are several other such examples of frauds yet many remain in school textbooks.

Darwin expressed doubts and problematic areas throughout his book *"On the Origin of the Species."* In fact one whole chapter is dedicated to irreconcilable problems with the theory of evolution. In the sixth chapter, *Difficulties on Theory*, he writes, "Long before having arrived at this part of my work, a crowd of difficulties will have occurred to the reader. Some of them are so grave that to this day I can never reflect on them without being staggered."[1] In his chapter on instinct he conceded such simple instincts as bees making a beehive could be sufficient to overthrow my whole theory. He went on to say "And to think that the eye could evolve by natural selection seems, I freely confess, absurd in the highest possible degree." In his chapter on imperfections in the geological record he complained that the complete lack of fossil intermediates in all geological records was perhaps, quote, "the most obvious and gravest objection which can be urged against my theory."[1] In other words, he was at least honest enough to admit that it didn't make any sense.

Given no real evidence, some have turned so far as to falsify fossils and create fossil hoaxes with the claim that a major missing link was found. The Britannica Encyclopedia says that the Piltdown man was a fraud! An analysis was made to date the bones more precisely and it was discovered that the skull was human and the jaw was that of a monkey with the teeth filed in to make them look human. Both creatures had recently died, but the bones had been chemically treated to make them look old and tests revealed that the bones were not from the same animal. Shockingly, from 1912 until 1953; that's over forty years, all the "expert, highly educated, brilliant," evolutionists of the world who studied these bones were completely fooled. Over 500 students wrote their doctoral dissertations on the Piltdown man which was a fraud, but they were still awarded Ph.D. degrees from outstanding universities of the world! Must we believe that from 1912 until 1953, over forty years, the most brilliant evolutionists of the world who studied these bones were fooled by a practical joke? Are we expected to give up our faith in God's eternal and infallible Word that He is Creator and trust such men who call themselves "scientists" and yet cannot tell the difference between scientific facts and fakery? They received their doctoral dissertations on a fake...a doctorate of fakery!

In 1974 Donald Johannson discovered a set of fossils that were stated to be 40% complete in Ethiopia. At first it was considered to be a female that stood less than three and a half feet tall. Her skull was not found, but a portion of the lower jaw was, or so they thought. It was an exact copy of a full ape-like one. What is never mentioned is the fact that other fossils from the same strata and location have been found, and these have all been fully ape, with the cranial capacity in the range of a modern chimp of today. Johannson's claim that Lucy was "the most important find made by anyone in the history of the entire human race" was overrated. He claimed she was three million years old and diagrammed at the very "Y" of the phylum branch that separated man and ape.

The media made an immediate celebrity of Johannson and hailed him as a hero. He even got his own institute for human biology at Berkeley (Cal.) University. The find was dubbed the infamous "Lucy" but something wasn't quite right. Why were scientists not allowed to examine it, or even touch it, until 1982...almost a decade later? Could the delay have been due to the fact that biologists could find no distinguishable differences between Lucy and the present-day rainforest Chimpanzee you might see at the Zoo. Little attention is given to the fact that Lucy is only three and a half feet tall. Now that's one short woman! Detailed studies of the inner ear, skulls and bones have suggested that Lucy was not on her way to becoming human. Where she was found is just as important. Lucy was located in the same area where the. Australopithecus afarensis once thrived. There were literally hundreds of bones that were found of the Australopithecus afarensis, which is similar to the pygmy chimpanzee.

Back in 1891, a Dutch army doctor, Eugene Dubois, stationed in Java, reported finding one of the first "missing links" between man and animal. What he discovered was the top of a skull, three jaw teeth, and part of a thighbone however these were found more than 70 feet apart, and these were only three of what were hundreds of bones along a creek bank. Dr. Dubois took over a year of searching and kept only three! It wasn't until after completing his military service that Dubois kept the bones in a trunk at home. He sent pencil drawings to various evolutionary leaders and museums of the world who eagerly welcomed his "scientific" proof. Perhaps he never followed up with that request because he had doubts about their authenticity, since he was the only one who had ever examined them.

Java Ape-Man or "Pithecanthropus erectus" is translated as "the ape-man that walks upright" but was he an actual ape-man? Biologists and evolutionists accepted his statement in faith, as "proof positive." Without question, they rather arrogantly declared to the world that the Ape-Man was 750,000 years old but it was only then that many of the leading scientists eagerly went to Doctor Dubois's Holland home to see for themselves those amazing bones. Dubois turned them away at his door. The story ends after about thirty-five years, when the scientific world demanded to see and evaluate the bones for themselves. Twenty-four European scientists eventually did meet to study the bones. Ten said they were the bones of an ape; seven said they came from a man; and seven said they were not the bones of a missing link. Dubois finally admitted that the bones were probably from an ape but the Java Ape-Man has been paraded in museums and high school and college text books the world over as the "missing link" between man and animals, allegedly proving evolution! Since there are far too many fossils labeled "missing links" to cover in one book, and these fossils contain inerrant problems, here are a couple of more examples of fossil phonies.

Ramapithecus: This was once widely regarded as the ancestor of humans, it has now been realized that it is merely an extinct type of orangutan (an ape).

Homo habilis: There is a growing consensus among most paleoanthropologists that this category actually includes bits and pieces of various other types an animals such as Australopithecus and Homo erectus. It is therefore an "invalid taxon." That is, it never existed as such.

There is no fossil evidence that man is the product of evolution. Could it be that the missing links are still missing because they simply do not exist? Regardless, discussing a newly discovered "missing link" seems ridiculous when there is no chain to begin with. One link does not make a chain.

1 http://www.literature.org, Charles Darwin, Origins of Species, Chapters 6 & 9, Difficulties on Theory and On the Imperfection of the Geological Records. Darwin's quotes located on e-book at:http://literature.org/authors/darwin-charles/ the-origin-of-species/ chapter-06.html, http://www.literature.org /authors/darwin-charles/the- origin-of-species/chapter-09.html

2 David B. Kitts. PhD (Zoology) Head Curator of the Department of Geology at the Stoval Museum. Genuine Knowledge, D.B. Kitts, 2006, University of Oklahoma. (Evolution, vol. 28, p. 467).

3 Colin Patterson, personal communication. Luther Sunderland, Darwin's Enigma: Fossils and Other Problems, 4th edition, 1988, (p. 88-90).

4 N. Heribert Nilsson, botanist, evolutionist and professor at Lund University in Sweden. as quoted in Arthur C. Custance, The Earth Before Man, Part II, Doorway Papers, no. 20, 1994. Ontario, Canada: Doorway Publications. (p. 51).

5 http://dailynightly.msnbc.msn.com/archive/2009/05/19/1937065. aspx 6 http://www.plosone.org/article/info:doi/10.1371/journal.pone. 0005723

CHAPTER ELEVEN

Are Carbon-14 Dating Methods Accurate or Reliable?

There are major issues with the reliability of Radiocarbon dating, which is defined as a radiometric dating method which uses naturally occurring radioisotope carbon-14. This is used to determine the age of carbonaceous materials, whether animal, vegetable or mineral and sometimes used in dating rock. What they do is come up with a "guesstimate" which is given in radiocarbon years (before present). Tests are said to have marginal errors of up to sixty-thousand years.[1] The rate of error skyrockets when testing is performed on non-organic materials, like rock. Carbon-14 dating methods are customarily used for dating the age of the earth, its various strata, and its fossils. Often, the results are highly questionable, since the radiocarbon years can differ radically, thus, the radiometric techniques used to date something may not be as reliable as scientists once thought.

Age estimates on a given geological stratum by using different radiometric methods have often differed radically from one another; sometimes by hundreds of millions of years. The problem lies within the long-term radiological 'clock' at the sub-atomic level of matter. Has the radiological clock remained constant for the matter? Are there causative factors that inhibit the accuracy of this radiological "clock?"

The uncertainties inherent in radiometric dating are disturbing to geologist and evolutionists W.D. Stansfield, Ph.D., Instructor of Biology at California Polytech State University, in the Science of Evolution (Macmillan Publishers, Oct. 1987). Here are two examples:

"When the blood of a seal, freshly killed at McMurdo Sound in the Antarctic was tested by carbon-14, it showed the seal had died 1,300 years ago." According to W. Dort Jr., Ph. D. Geology, Professor, University of Kansas, who was quoted in Antarctic Journal of the United States, in February, 1971: "The hair on the Chekurovka mammoth was found to have a carbon-14 age of 26,000 years but the peaty soil in which it was preserved was found to have a carbon-14 dating of only 5,600 years" (Radiocarbon Journal, Vol. 8, 1966.).

Carbon has unique properties that are essential for life on earth. Familiar to us as the black substance in charred wood, as diamonds, and the graphite in "lead" pencils, carbon comes in several forms, or isotopes. One rare form has atoms that are 14 times as heavy as hydrogen atoms: carbon-14, 14C, or radiocarbon. Carbon-14 is created when cosmic rays knock neutrons out of atomic nuclei in the upper atmosphere. These displaced neutrons, now moving fast, hit ordinary nitrogen (14N) at lower altitudes, converting it into 14C. Unlike common carbon (12C), 14C is unstable and slowly decays, changing it back to nitrogen and releasing energy. This instability makes it radioactive.

Age estimates which are obviously wrong or contradictory are sometimes produced. For example, new rock in the form of hardened lava flows produced estimated ages as great as 3 million to 3.5 billion years, when they were actually less than 200 years old. A popular and supposedly foolproof method was used on two lava flows in the Grand Canyon that should be ideal for radioactive age estimation. The results were similarly bad. Young basalt rock at the Canyon's top produced an age estimate 270 million years older than ancient basalt rock at the Canyon's bottom. Clearly the rock at the top of the Grand Canyon should have been millions of years older than the rocks at the bottom but the results were just the opposite and were certainly wrong. The problem seems to arise from basic wrong assumptions in the method (rubidium-strontium isochron). Ordinary carbon (12C) is found in the carbon dioxide (CO2) in the air, which is taken up by plants, which in turn are eaten by animals and so a bone, or a leaf or a tree, or even a piece of wooden furniture, contains carbon. When the 14C has been formed, like ordinary carbon (12C), it combines with oxygen to produce carbon dioxide (14CO2), and so it also gets cycled through the cells of plants and animals. Now here's the great discrepancy. It's possible to take a sample of air, count how many 12C atoms there are for every 14C atom, and calculate the 14C/12C ratio. Because 14C is so well mixed with 12C, we expect to find that this ratio would be the same if we sample a leaf from a tree, or one of your finger nails. In living things, although 14C atoms are constantly changing back to 14N (soluble nitrogen), they are still exchanging carbon with their surroundings, so the mixture remains about the same as in the atmosphere. However, as soon as a plant or animal dies, the 14C atoms which decay are no longer replaced, so the amount of 14C in that once-living organism decreases as time goes on. In other words, the 14C/12C ratio gets smaller. This so-called "atomic clock" starts ticking the moment something dies.

The point is that carbon dating was designed for once living organisms, not for non-organic, non-living matter, which have vastly differing 14C/12C propensities. Given that, there remains a high rate of error in which even organic matter can produce wrong estimates. Rocks however, have a fairly constant rate of 14C breaking down into 12C over thousands of years. The rate is similar, whether it is igneous, sedimentary, or metamorphic however, the unreliability of carbon dating rocks is seen when adjacent rocks test radically different in dates.

Rocks accumulate C14 atoms from surrounding rocks, plants, animals, water or by other means but they can just as easily lose C-14 atoms from floods, burials and cataclysmic events (i.e., volcanism).

Natural catastrophes (water, fire, pressure) can reset the atomic clock in matter, restoring the original 14C/12C ratio. This would tend to make it appear to be much younger than it actually is and if it's too young, you can bet that they will throw out that estimate, and try again and again, until they find a date which more closely fits their idea. My question is: "Has matters atomic clock remained constant?" No one can say with certainty. Catastrophes can just as easily skew the isotropic C14 to C12 ratio test the other way too; giving estimates much older than they actually are. Because of their bias, these results they do accept are almost always, without question, the oldest date estimated. Hundreds of times, carbon dating of rocks and animals has proven to be highly unreliable and inaccurate. Animal and human skulls, fossilized or not, are subject to the very same loss or gain in C14 atoms as rocks are. Plant and animal fossilized remains were found under the lava and ash flow of Mt. Saint Helen's 1980 eruption and it took less than 30 years, not millions of years as most people assume is necessary for fossilization to occur.[2] The remains of the animals and plants were obviously not ancient but the cataclysmic event may have created such pressure and heat, that fossilization occurred in less than twenty-five years. Scientists have produced fossilization in less than ten years in one controlled laboratory environment using chicken bones.[3]

One thing that carbon dating is useful for is dating documents, paper, ancient scrolls, or papyruses. This might be the best use of carbon-14 dating. Scientists arrive at a "date" dependent upon a chain of assumptions. With documents they have some type of archeological or historical data to consider in there dating estimates but the validity of the calculated date in rocks, can be no stronger than the weakest link (weakest assumption) used in the calculation. Here are the chief assumptions made by scientists when dating matter, and why using carbon dating methods on non-organic matter is the primary concern associated with it:

Scientists generally assume the material being measured had no original "daughter" element(s) in it, or they assume the amount can be accurately estimated. For example, they may assume that all of the lead in a rock was produced by the decay of its uranium. The problem is that one can almost never know with absolute certainty how much radioactive or daughter substance was present at the start. Scientists tend to assume that the material being measured has been in a closed system. It has often been wrongly assumed that no outside factors altered the normal ratios in the material, adding or subtracting any of the elements involved. However, the age estimate can be thrown off considerably if the radioactive element or the daughter element is leached in or leached out of the sample. There are evidences that this could be a significant problem. Simple things such as groundwater movement can carry radioactive material or the daughter element into or out of rock. Rocks must be carefully tested to determine what outside factors might have changed their content but they don't normally test for this!

Scientists also assume that the rate of decomposition has always remained constant or absolutely constant but how can one be certain that decay rates have been constant over their estimated "billions of years?" Scientific measurements of decay rates have only been conducted since the time of the Curies in the early 1900s and there is some evidence that the rate of radioactive decay can change. If the decay rates have ever been higher in the past, then relatively young rocks would mistakenly be dated and then classified as being much older.

The age of our globe is presently thought to be around 4.5 billion years, based on radio-decay rates of uranium and thorium, but scientists have not found a way to determine the exact age of the Earth directly from Earth rocks because Earth's oldest rocks have been recycled and destroyed by the process of plate tectonics. Now scientists realize that radio-decay rates are not as constant as they had previously thought, nor are they immune to environmental influences and so carbon dating methods, at best, can yield significant margins of error. The next time you hear that carbon dating has established something as millions or billions of years old, remember that they are making a subjective "guesstimate." No one knows precisely and the margins of error may exceed a thousand percent. That is one huge margin for error. And that margin for error is enough to leave room for doubt amid the subjective speculation of dating "guesstimates."

1 http://en.wikipedia.org/wiki/Radiocarbon_dating

2 Dr. H. Coffin, 'Erect floating stumps in Spirit Lake, Washington,' Geology Magazine, May 1983.

3 G.R. Hill. Chemical Technology, May 1972. (p. 296).

CHAPTER TWELVE

The Universe: Young or Old, Finite or Infinite?

All that scientists have are theories in explaining the age of the universe. The vast majority of scientists, but not all modern secular ("big bang") theorists, have cosmologies that agree. Science is in the business of making arbitrary assumptions (theories) without having conclusive scientific evidence. One such belief is that the universe has no boundaries; no edge and no center. In this assumed universe, every galaxy would be surrounded by galaxies spread evenly in all directions (on a large enough scale); therefore, all the net gravitational forces cancel each other out. But if the universe and matter are finite and if the universe has boundaries or an ending, then there must necessarily be a net gravitational effect toward the center. One example would be that clocks at the edge of this outward boundary of the universe would be running at different rates to clocks on the earth than those places toward the center and time would be vastly different if you were traveling at the speed of light.

You would think there would be time-rate differentials from the center of the universe than there would be at the extreme outer edges of the universe, if such an ending or edge does exist. If the universe is finite, then the time at this outward boundary could differ from the time at the center; for time may be flying exponentially at the outer boundaries, while in the center, time may be at a much slower rate, relative to the outer boundaries. Based upon what we know, it would be reasonable to assume that there is an ending of the physical universe. The further away the galaxies are from us, the faster they are moving away from us. And it is still accelerating at ever increasing speeds. This means that there was a time in which it was slower in moving away, and had not filled in all the spaces in the universe yet, compared to where it is now. Since it is growing exponentially faster in moving outward, could it have been much slower when it was nearer the beginning stages? An analogy would be when you hear a train whistle...as it passes, its frequency changes. The sound goes down in pitch, getting stretched out...stretching out further and further as it travels away. We are not hearing the original sound that we heard when the train whistle was right in front of us. When it becomes very faint, it takes a few seconds for us to even hear it. What we hear at that moment is already seconds behind the original blast although at the train it is heard immediately.

There appears to be observational evidence that the universe has expanded in the past and continues to expand today. The Bible uses similarly descriptive terms where at creation, God is said to have "stretched out the heavens."[1] Other descriptions were that God "spread out" the heavens. If the universe is not much bigger than we can observe, and if it was only 50 times smaller in the past than it is now (which is was), then scientific deduction based on gravitation relative to the center means it had to have expanded out of a previous state in which it was surrounded by an event horizon (a condition known technically as a "white hole" which is a black hole running in reverse, something permitted by the equations of equilibrium.[2] As matter passed out of this event horizon, the horizon itself had to shrink—eventually to nothing. Therefore, at one point this earth (relative to a point far away from it) would have been virtually frozen in time. An observer on earth would not in any way feel different. "Billions of years" would be available (in the frame of reference within which it is traveling in deep space) for light to reach the earth, for stars to age, etc.—while less than one ordinary day is passing on earth. This massive gravitational time dilation would seem to be a scientific inevitability if a bounded universe expanded significantly.

In one sense, if observers on earth at that particular time could have looked out and "seen" the speed with which light was moving toward them out in space, it would have appeared as if it were traveling many times faster than a constant c. Galaxies would also appear to be rotating faster. However, if an observer in deep space was out there measuring the speed of light; to him it would still only be traveling at c. If the galaxy is spreading out (and it is), the outer parts would be moving out faster than the center part (and it is). The results are that the outer most galaxies are traveling the fastest while the inner most galaxies traveling the slowest.

You would think that this motion would have a considerable amount of effect on the movement of time, particularly on the outward fringes of the universe. At the extreme fringes, time could be measured at less than a nanosecond in contrast to the central most parts of the universe, which might take hundreds of years. Job (38:7) speaks of the cosmos and all of creation to have been instantaneous, saying that "the morning stars [angels] sang together, and all the sons of God [angels] shouted for joy." Now if God used evolution over eons of time, then the angels had one looooonnnnnggg shout by anyone's definition.

This cosmology is based upon mathematics and physics which are totally accepted by cosmologists (general relativity), and it accepts (along with virtually all physicists) that there has been expansion in the past (said to be from some tiny, theoretical starting point). So the arbitrary starting point which the Big Bang theory holds to is to use the unbounded cosmos idea which states the universe has no end and if it has no end, we must presume they believe it had no beginning either. Whether it is called the Big Bang, the Steady State theory, or whatever, it appears to violate the 2nd and 3rd Laws of Thermodynamics (among others), and Einstein's Theory of Relativity ($E=mc2$); which demands a cause for every effect.

Part of the way in which the universe is dated is by the speed of light and the distant star light's time needed to reach the earth. The distance that the light has to travel to earth is used to configure the years. Many scientists, physicists, and astronomers claim that since the stars are so many light years away, it had to take billions of years for the light to reach and be observed on earth. However, if the universe was created, would God not create the heavens without light already being visible from the earth? He said let there be light and at that very moment it was! Immediately one conceives. What could delay what God had spoken into immediacy? Reading Genesis one and two, among other Scriptures in the Old Testament, it is obvious that star light was already being seen on the earth at creation, thus, it would be logical to assume that the light was created at the same time as the universe...in full maturity! That is having already been being viewed by humans. Why would God create the universe and then wait billions of years for the light to reach the earth?

Genesis one plainly indicates that God spoke and it existed! Creation was instant fiat! Scientific theories cannot explain what caused matter to come from nothingness. These theories come with no conclusive proof. String Theory, Steady-State Theory, Big Bang Theory, etc. do not explain the cause of the effect (material universe). From the language of the Bible, it is clear that the universe was created an already mature state. Adam and Eve were also created in full maturity, as adults. They were old enough to marry and bear children and old enough to "keep the garden"(Gen. 2:15). They didn't have to wait for a harvest either since there was already fruit on the trees (Gen. 2:16), another indication that the earth was already fully mature when created.

By all readings, even the creatures were fully mature but so was the physical world. Mountains and valleys appeared simultaneously. Adam named all the animals. He didn't name baby calves, but cattle, or chicks but chickens, not ducklings but already flying fowl, and not single-celled amoebas after the amoeba kind (Gen. 2:19-20). This new cosmology seems to explain the observations that the Hubble Telescope has been recording, like the progressive red-shift and the cosmic microwave background radiation, without compromising the data or the biblical record of a young earth. This new cosmology is not the creationist's alternative to the Big Bang theory. It is simply a recognition that the Theory of General Relativity does not permit time to exist without matter and that a fully mature creation was already in place in the beginning. It acknowledges the fact that the speed of light has not remained constant over the last one-hundred-fifty years and carbon-14 dating methods are notorious for their margins of error.

My oldest son had why-itis. Why is the sun yellow, why doesn't it burn up, why did this happen, how come that is? I never said to my children "because that's what I learned." They wanted direct answers. Neither should we so easily consent with a theoretical explanation that lacks conclusive proof and that leaves God out of the explanation. Science by nature is always digging, not satisfied with the status quo. Science means knowledge and knowledge is always growing, throwing out old findings and taking in new findings. No one need apologize when challenging textbook science, asking for conclusive evidence about scientific suppositions, and questioning conventional acceptance of theoretical suppositions? We all ought to be humbled by just how much knowledge there appears to be in the universe. Expanding the mind, questioning contemporary thought, and asking a lot of questions are healthy. It's okay. That is actually the part of science where the most progression is made.

We don't really know exactly how old the earth is but does it really matter? God created it and that's all that matters. We know that the theory evolution is so full of holes that it cannot possible hold water. It cannot be observed, it cannot be tested, it cannot be repeated, and it cannot be falsified, all of which makes it impossible to pass through the scientific method. Evolution will always remain a theory and will never become a law of science. It actually takes more faith to believe that everything came from nothing than it does to believe there was a cause for the effect of the universe and life. Creation provides the cause for the effect of the universe; and it does not conflict with the present, empirical, cosmological scientific evidence that we hold today. Evolution can never be proved but please don't think that you can debate or argue someone with evidence into the kingdom of heaven.

No one was or ever will be debated into eternal life. No one has or will ever be brow beaten into submitting to God. Only the Holy Spirit can bring a person to repentance, confession of their sins, to see their need for forgiveness, and to place their trust in Christ. I hope I have given you good reasons to see why we can believe that there is a God and that He does exist, that He is the Creator and that His Word, the Bible, can be believed. I would rather lose a debate and win a soul than win a debate and lose a soul, not that I save anyone because God alone saves. My prayer is that you can now "be prepared to give an answer to everyone who asks you to give the reason for the hope that you have. But do this with gentleness and respect" (1 Pet 3:15) but let me emphasize, do "this with gentleness and respect."

1 Genesis 1:1; Ecclesiastes 3:11; Isaiah 26:4; Romans 1:20; 1 Timothy 1:17; and Hebrews 11:3, Isaiah 42:5; Jeremiah 10:12; Zechariah 12:1.

2 D. Russell Humphreys, Starlight and Time (Green Forest, AR: Master Books, 1994). An on-line archive of the debate surrounding Dr. Humphreys' starlight research can be found off-site at:http://www.trueorigin.org/ca_rh_03.htm

Blind Chance or Intelligent Design? Copyright © 2014 by Jack Wellman
All rights reserved. No part of this book may be reproduced or transmitted in any form or by any means without written permission from the author. To contact the author, please email him at: jackwellman@hotmail.com 98 pages
ISBN 978-0-557-09307-6
Printed in USA

Other books from this author include *Do Babies Go to Heaven, Teaching Children the Gospel; How to Raise Godly Children,* and *The Great Omission; Reaching the Lost for the Great Commission*

Made in the USA
Monee, IL
02 October 2020